NO FUSS

MATHS
PHOTOCOPIABLES
AGES 5-7

LEVELS 1-3

- **Levelled and linked to the curriculum**

- **Stand-alone photocopiable activities**

- **Ideal for mixed-age classes**

Compiled by Roger Smith

CONTRIBUTORS

Text © **Catherine Musto and Marion Cranmer**: 15, 16, 29, 30, 34, 35, 42, 43, 46, 54, 62, 63, 75, 76, 77, 78, 84, 90, 94, 95, 96

Text © **John Davis and Sonia Tibbatts**: 26, 27, 28, 44, 45, 53, 55, 56, 57, 58, 91, 92, 93

Text © **Rose Griffiths**: 17, 18, 19, 20, 31, 32, 33, 41, 47, 48, 49, 50, 51, 52, 59, 60, 61, 64, 65, 66, 67, 68, 69, 70

Text © **Leonie McKinnon**: 81, 82, 83, 87, 88, 89, 97, 98, 99, 101, 102, 104, 105, 106, 109, 110, 111, 112, 113, 114, 115, 116, 117, 118, 119, 120, 121, 122, 123, 124, 125, 126, 127

Text © **Barbara Raper**: 21, 22, 23, 24, 25, 36, 37, 38, 39, 40, 71, 72, 73, 74, 79, 80, 85, 86, 100, 103, 107, 108

CONSULTANT EDITOR

Roger Smith

ASSISTANT EDITOR

Wendy Tse

DESIGNERS

Lapiz Digital

COVER DESIGN

Anna Oliwa

ILLUSTRATORS

Illustration © **Caroline Ewen**: 97, 98, 99, 101, 102, 104, 105, 106, 109, 110, 111, 112, 113, 114, 115, 116, 117, 118, 119, 120, 121, 122, 123, 124, 125, 126, 127

Illustration © **Louise Gardner**: 81, 82, 83, 87, 88, 89

Illustration © **Gloria**: 16, 29, 30, 35, 42, 43, 46, 54, 62, 63, 75, 76, 77, 95, 96

Illustration © **Sarah Hedley**: 31, 32, 47, 64, 65, 100, 103, 107, 108

Illustration © **Helen Herbert**: 33, 85, 86

Illustration © **Kim Lane**: 59, 60, 61, 66, 67, 68, 69, 70, 71, 72, 73, 74, 79, 80

Illustration © **Mary Lonsdale**: 17, 18, 19, 20, 21, 22, 23, 24, 25, 36, 37, 38, 39, 40, 41, 48, 49, 50, 51, 52

Illustration © **Hilary McElderry**: 15, 34, 78, 84, 90, 94

Illustration © **Liz Thomas**: 26, 27, 44, 53, 55, 57, 58, 92, 93

Text and illustration copyright in individual pages as per acknowledgements.
Compilation © 2006 Scholastic Ltd

Every effort has been made to trace all the copyright owners of material but there were a few cases where an author or illustrator was untraceable. Scholastic will be happy to correct any omissions in future printings.

Published by Scholastic Ltd
Villiers House
Clarendon Avenue
Leamington Spa
Warwickshire
CV32 5PR

www.scholastic.co.uk

Designed using Adobe InDesign

Printed by Bell & Bain Ltd, Glasgow

1 2 3 4 5 6 7 8 9   6 7 8 9 0 1 2 3 4 5

British Library Cataloguing-in-Publication Data

A catalogue record for this book is available from the British Library.

ISBN 0-439-96550-0

ISBN 978-0439-96550-7

Extracts from the National Numeracy Strategy reproduced under the terms of HMSO Guidance Note 8. © Crown copyright.

Reproduction of coins by permission of The Royal Mint © Crown copyright.

Photocopiable pages and original teachers' notes first published in *Surveys, First fractions, First number patterns, Measuring, Money, Numbers to 20, Numbers to 50* and *Shapes and patterns* (all first published 1993) from the Essentials for Maths series, and *Exploring shape and space* (1996), *Maths* (1992), *Maths puzzles* (1994) and *Measurement skills* (1996) from the Teacher Timesavers series.

www.scholastic.co.uk

CONTENTS

CONTENTS

INTRODUCTION

The main purpose of this book is to provide teachers with a set of easy-to-use, varied and stimulating activities, which are linked to the National Numeracy Strategy for England and the Scottish National Guidelines for Mathematics 5-14. These activities will not only provide back-up learning materials for individuals, pairs and groups but can also be used as extension work to support other resources and, because they are graded in levels, be used as part of any assessment process. More than anything, however, the emphasis is on practical activities and games, which should be linked to plenty of experience with the kinds of apparatus that are easily available in the classroom.

Using a wide range of resources is essential to meaningful learning in mathematics. By using these activities you will be able to:

- introduce new skills and concepts
- encourage children to practise skills in the manipulation of numbers and symbols
- consolidate and reinforce a mathematical concept
- demonstrate the possibility of using ideas and information in a new situation
- add elements of flexibility to your maths teaching
- gain some indication of the children's current level of attainment.

The various sections of the National Numeracy Strategy, such as Calculations and Measures, shape and space, and of the Scottish National Guidelines for Mathematics 5-14, such as Information handling and Shape, position and movement, exist as discrete elements but there is also some overlap. This is also the case with some of the activities in this book, which may be placed in one section but could equally be used in another. It is worth familiarising yourself with them. Each activity has also been allocated a level of difficulty but you will know your children and what they are or are not capable of completing; it is possible that some of the levels and activities can be adjusted to fit individuals or groups.

Children's understanding can be developed if they can communicate their ideas verbally. Discussing mathematical concepts helps them to consolidate their knowledge, to learn different ways of thinking and to clarify their thoughts. Wherever possible there should be follow-up discussions between children or between children and teacher.

Finally, all the activities should be interesting and encourage children to both learn the maths they need to know and to enjoy it. For some children maths can be a challenge and there are activities here that will help them rise to the challenge. For some children maths is an exciting adventure where they always want to learn more so at the end of most of the activities there are suggestions for further work, which should mean that even in the busiest and most mixed-ability classroom there should be something for everyone.

Page	Activity	Objective	Teachers' notes	National Numeracy Strategy links	Scottish Curriculum links	KS1 Levels
page 15	Bags of apples	To begin to count reliably.	Children who have difficulty may use counters to match the apples in each bag.	Counting, properties of numbers and number sequences: To count reliably.	Number, money and measurement – Level A	AT2 Level 1
page 16	Sets	To begin to count reliably.	The children could draw the sets rather than stick them in their books if this is more appropriate.	Counting, properties of numbers and number sequences: To count reliably.	Number, money and measurement – Level A	AT2 Level 1
page 17	Peanuts	To count reliably at least 20 objects.	Counters could be used to match the peanuts for those children who find the activity difficult.	Counting, properties of numbers and number sequences: Count reliably to 20. Place value and ordering: Read and write numerals to 20.	Number, money and measurement – Level A	AT2 Level 1
pages 18, 19 and 20	Legs to twenty	To count reliably at least 20 objects.	This game works best if it is copied onto thin card and if it is played with two people. The instructions can be made into a mini-book, or be folded into a zigzag book. Ensure that the children know how many legs each animal has before they begin.	Counting, properties of numbers and number sequences: Count reliably to 20. Place value and ordering: Read and write numerals to 20.	Number, money and measurement – Level A	AT2 Level 1
page 21	Missing numbers	To order numbers to at least 20.	The activity can be used as it is or cut into strips. The children could follow the activity up by making their own strips.	Counting, properties of numbers and number sequences: Count on and back in ones. Place value and ordering: Order numbers to 20.	Number, money and measurement – Level A	AT2 Level 1
page 22	Three in a line	To order numbers to at least 20.	Children should be encouraged to make their own puzzles and to ask a partner to find the missing numbers.	Counting, properties of numbers and number sequences: Count on and back in ones. Place value and ordering: Order numbers to 20.	Number, money and measurement – Level A	AT2 Level 1
page 23	Telephones	To order numbers to at least 20.	Children may wish to compare the sequence of numbers on a real telephone with those on a calculator or on a PC keyboard.	Counting, properties of numbers and number sequences: Describe and extend number sequences. Place value and ordering: Position numbers on a number track.	Number, money and measurement – Level A	AT2 Level 1
page 24	Colouring numbers	To recognise even numbers up to 20 and the pattern they make in a sequence of numbers.	Compulsive 'colourers' may need to be told that only some of the numbers are going to be coloured in.	Counting, properties of numbers and number sequences: To begin to recognise even numbers to 20.	Number, money and measurement – Level A	AT2 Level 1
page 25	Dice patterns	To describe and extend number sequences.	They may be able to discover for themselves that the opposite sides of dice, when added together, total 7.	Counting, properties of numbers and number sequences: Describe and extend number sequences. Estimating: Give a sensible estimate.	Number, money and measurement – Level A	AT2 Level 1
page 26	Snakes and ladders	To count on and back from a starting number.	The children should have access to counting materials, such as cubes or counters, and be encouraged to discuss the number patterns.	Counting, properties of numbers and number sequences: Counting in steps of 2, 3, 4, and 5.	Number, money and measurement – Level B	AT2 Level 2

Page	Activity	Objective	Teachers' notes	National Numeracy Strategy links	Scottish Curriculum links	KS1 Levels
page 27	The puzzled postie	To count on and back in twos in odd and even numbers.	Talk about how most streets will have even house numbers on one side and odd house numbers on the opposite side. This activity can be extended by using different numbers and children can be encouraged to make up their own list of house numbers.	Counting, properties of numbers and number sequences: Counting in steps of 2,3,4, and 5, and to recognise odd and even numbers.	Number, money and measurement – Level B	AT2 Level 2
page 28	Arrowgraphs	To count on in threes and fours and begin to understand the concept of doubling.	In the first two examples, all the numbers are visited once but not in one string; the third example has several short chains and not all the numbers are visited. Children should be encouraged to complete the final part of this activity and to use it with a friend.	Counting, properties of numbers and number sequences: Counting on. Place value and ordering: Order numbers.	Number, money and measurement – Level B	AT2 Level 2
page 29	Number cards	To partition two-digit numbers and order them.	Children should be encouraged to complete the final part of this activity and to use it with a friend.	Counting, properties of numbers and number sequences: Counting on. Place value and ordering: Order numbers.	Number, money and measurement – Level B	AT2 Level 2
page 30	Three-digit numbers	To begin to partition numbers into hundreds, tens and units.	This can be extended by using 0 and allowing each digit to be used more than once.	Place value and ordering: Order larger numbers and begin to partition them.	Number, money and measurement – Level B	AT2 Level 2/3
page 31	Number spiral	To count reliably in different ways.	The number spiral can be used for all kinds of games that involve counting backwards and forwards.	Counting, properties of numbers and number sequences: Describe and extend simple number sequences. Place value and ordering: Order whole numbers and position them on a number line.	Number, money and measurement – Level B	AT2 Level 2
page 32	Spiral games	To count reliably in different ways.	These are some ideas for using the number spiral and need to be cut out so that they can be used separately.	Counting, properties of numbers and number sequences: Describe and extend simple number sequences. Place value and ordering: Order whole numbers and position them on a number line.	Number, money and measurement – Level B	AT2 Level 2
page 33	Halves	To begin to use and understand halves accurately.	Talk to the children about the precise use of the term 'half' – in maths it means to split something into two pieces which are exactly the same size.	Fractions: Begin to recognise and find one half of shapes.	Number, money and measurement – Level B	AT2 Level 2
page 34	Halves	To begin to use and understand halves accurately.	This page needs to be copied several times so that children can cut the shapes into halves in different ways and it can be extended to quarters.	Fractions: Begin to recognise and find one half of shapes.	Number, money and measurement – Level B	AT2 Level 2
page 35	Dominoes	To add two numbers together.	Provide enough sets of dominoes for all the children. The children could sort the dominoes for the different totals of spots.	Understanding addition and subtraction: Understand the operation of addition.	Number, money and measurement – Level A	AT2 Level 1
pages 36 and 37	Crabs – 1 and 2	To understand the addition and subtraction facts for the number 5.	The children will need to understand addition and subtraction facts for the number 5. Many children will be able to write their findings as calculations using + and –.	Understanding addition and subtraction: Understand the operation of addition and subtraction; begin to use + and – signs.	Number, money and measurement – Level A	AT2 Level 1

Page	Activity	Objective	Teachers' notes	National Numeracy Strategy links	Scottish Curriculum links	KS1 Levels
pages 38 and 39	Hedgehogs – 1 and 2	To understand and begin to record addition facts.	Children should be encouraged to write the calculations on separate paper as a simple calculation without the drawings of hedgehogs, for example 5 + 3 = 8.	Understanding addition and subtraction: Begin to use the + sign.	Number, money and measurement – Level A	AT2 Level 1
page 40	Number 10	To add numbers to total up to 10.	Provide the children with counters if necessary. Similar sheets could be made for other numbers.	Rapid recall of addition and subtraction facts: To know by heart the addition facts for numbers with a total of 10.	Number, money and measurement – Level A	AT2 Level 1
page 41	Up and downstairs	To add numbers to total up to 10.	Provide the children with counters if necessary. Similar sheets could be made for other numbers.	Rapid recall of addition and subtraction facts: To know by heart the addition facts for numbers with a total of 10.	Number, money and measurement – Level A	AT2 Level 1
page 42	Difference pairs	To begin to understand some of the vocabulary related to subtraction.	Provide the children with counters or buttons. Make sure that the children complete the final section of this activity.	Understanding addition and subtraction: Understand the operation of addition and subtraction, and use the related vocabulary. Mental calculation strategies (+ and –): Find a small difference between a pair of numbers.	Number, money and measurement – Level B	AT2 Level 2
page 43	Jumping frogs	To understand more about calculations involving + and –.	Some children may need to use counting materials for this activity to work out how to get the frogs from one lily-pad to another.	Understanding addition and subtraction: Understand that subtraction is the inverse of addition.	Number, money and measurement – Level B	AT2 Level 2
page 44	Pyram-adds	To begin to understand addition involving larger numbers.	Some children will be able to work with larger numbers and others may still need counting materials. The children may want to establish 'rules' for using numbers in the pyram-add diagram. It is not possible to have a total that is more than 80, which is the maximum.	Understanding addition and subtraction: Begin to add more than two numbers and numbers with two digits.	Number, money and measurement – Level B	AT2 Level 2/3
page 45	Reducing squares	To practise subtraction skills.	Encourage the children to try corner numbers of all sizes.	Mental calculation strategies (+ and –): Find a small difference between a pair of numbers.	Number, money and measurement – Level B	AT2 Level 2/3
page 46	Buns for bears	To develop an understanding of multiplication and division.	Counters or cubes will need to be used with this activity. An extra bun is included in the basket so the children will need to consider how to share the bun between four.	Understanding multiplication and division: Understand the operation of multiplication as repeated addition; begin to understand division as sharing.	Number, money and measurement – Level B	AT2 Level 2/3
page 47	Marbles	To develop an understanding of multiplication and division.	This is a versatile activity. Think before copying it and change the number in the speech bubble to make it easier or more difficult.	Understanding multiplication and division: Understand the operation of multiplication as repeated addition.	Number, money and measurement – Level B	AT2 Level 2/3
pages 48 and 49	Bus sums 1 and 2	To use addition to solve simple problems.	Before using this activity make sure the children understand and can complete simple mental problems such as: *There were seven people on the bus and five more got on – how many were on the bus?* Some children will need to use counters.	Reasoning about numbers or shapes: Solve simple mathematical problems.	Problem-solving and enquiry – Level A	AT1 Level 1
page 50	Fruit and Tins	To use addition to solve simple problems.	This page makes two activities. Children can make up another sheet of their own to try on a friend.	Reasoning about numbers or shapes: Solve simple mathematical problems.	Problem-solving and enquiry – Level A	AT1 Level 1

Page	Activity	Objective	Teachers' notes	National Numeracy Strategy links	Scottish Curriculum links	KS1 Levels
page 51	Seeds	To use addition to solve problems and begin to explain the relationship of addition to multiplication.	It is much better to use sunflower seeds – but counters will do.	Reasoning about numbers or shapes: Solve simple mathematical problems.	Problem-solving and enquiry – Level A	AT1 Level 1
page 52	Seed sums	To use addition and subtraction to solve problems.	It is much better to use sunflower seeds – but counters will do.	Reasoning about numbers or shapes: Solve mathematical problems.	Problem-solving and enquiry – Level A/B	AT1 Level 2
page 53	Number routes	To use addition to solve more difficult problems.	Using scrap paper would be useful. It is important to discuss this activity with those children who are able to complete it. Answers: $4 + 3 + 7 = 14; 9 + 3 + 7 + 5 = 24; 3 + 5 = 8$.	Reasoning about numbers or shapes: Solve mathematical problems.	Problem-solving and enquiry – Level A/B	AT1 Level 2
page 54	Travelling by train	To begin to solve mathematical problems.	Try and make the activity harder by changing the number of people to put in the carriage to three.	Reasoning about numbers or shapes: Solve mathematical problems.	Problem-solving and enquiry – Level B	AT1 Level 2
page 55	Bull's-eye	To begin to solve mathematical problems.	Double and treble circles can be added to this activity. It is important to spend time discussing the scores.	Reasoning about numbers or shapes: Solve mathematical problems.	Problem-solving and enquiry – Level B	AT1 Level 2
page 56	Some sums	To begin to solve mathematical problems that involve addition, subtraction, multiplication and division.	This activity can be used with different totals and the numbers can be changed to practise other number operations.	Reasoning about numbers or shapes: Solve mathematical problems, recognise and predict from simple patterns and relationships.	Problem-solving and enquiry – Level B	AT1 Level 2
page 57	Magic squares	To solve problems involving reaching a specific total.	Don't forget to let the children devise their own magic squares. Some children should only be expected to complete the first example and then to try their own.	Reasoning about numbers or shapes: Solve mathematical problems, recognise and predict from simple patterns and relationships.	Problem-solving and enquiry – Level B	AT1 Level 3
page 58	Make 57	To add a series of numbers together to reach a specific total.	You could limit the total to a much lower number – just change the page before you photocopy it. Make sure the children understand the rules before they start.	Reasoning about numbers or shapes: Solve mathematical problems, recognise and predict from simple patterns and relationships.	Problem-solving and enquiry – Level B	AT1 Level 3
pages 59 and 60	The ten pence game and playing cards	To recognise and count money.	This activity is about recognising coins and counting money up to ten pence. Copying the game on to card and laminating it will make it last longer.	Problems involving 'real life', money or measures: Recognise coins and find totals.	Number, money and measurement – Level A	AT2 Level 1
page 61	Jumble toys	To recognise and count money.	Don't forget to have plenty of coins available.	Problems involving 'real life', money or measures: Recognise coins and find totals.	Number, money and measurement – Level A	AT2 Level 1
page 62	Money track	To find totals and work out an exact sum using small coins.	Laminating this game will make it look better and last longer. Include an element of probability by asking whether all the coins can be picked up if there is no time limit.	Problems involving 'real life', money or measures: Recognise coins and find totals.	Number, money and measurement – Level A	AT2 Level 1
page 63	Classroom shop	To find totals and work out how to pay an exact sum.	Children may need some guidance to help them work with manageable bills.	Problems involving 'real life', money or measures: Recognise all coins. Understanding addition and subtraction: Extend understanding of the operation of addition.	Number, money and measurement – Level A/B	AT2 Level 2

Page	Activity	Objective	Teachers' notes	National Numeracy Strategy links	Scottish Curriculum links	KS1 Levels
pages 64 and 65	Penny games: Guess and count; What's left? and Groups	To find totals by estimating and counting.	Don't forget to make sure that the children estimate first. It is much better if they use real money.	Problems involving 'real life', money or measures: Recognise all coins. Understanding addition and subtraction: Extend understanding of the operation of addition and subtraction.	Number, money and measurement – Level B	AT2 Level 2
page 66	Bus fares	To find totals and give change.	Don't forget to have plenty of coins available.	Problems involving 'real life', money or measures: Recognise all coins and work out which coins to pay.	Number, money and measurement – Level B	AT2 Level 2
pages 67 and 68	The fifty pence game and playing cards	To reach a specific total.	It is best to copy these pages onto thin card and laminate before you cut up the sheets.	Problems involving 'real life', money or measures: Recognise all coins and find totals.	Number, money and measurement – Level B	AT2 Level 2
pages 69 and 70	Count up to £1	To reach a specific total using groups of coins.	It is best to copy these pages onto thin card and laminate before you cut up the sheets. Use the pages to make a flip-book: cut the page into three strips along the horizontal dotted lines; collect the strips together so that the top strip from page 69 is the front cover and the last strip from page 70 is at the back; staple the book together above the solid line; cut along the vertical dotted lines on the four middle pages, to make the lift-up flaps.	Problems involving 'real life', money or measures: Recognise all coins and find totals.	Number, money and measurement – Level B	AT2 Level 2
pages 71 and 72	Holidays and Holiday homes	To organise information in a simple way.	This is a useful activity to introduce the children to 'tallying'. The children could either colour in all the pictures before the survey, or colour in the most popular choice. Some children may be able to develop their own surveys.	Organising and using data: Sort, classify and organise information in a simple way.	Information handling – Level A	AT4 Level 1
page 73	Choose a badge	To organise information in a simple way.	This is a useful activity to introduce the children to 'tallying'. The children could survey which is the most popular design in their table group and in the whole class. Some children may be able to develop their own surveys.	Organising and using data: Sort, classify and organise information in a simple way.	Information handling – Level A	AT4 Level 1
page 74	Choose your pets	To organise information in a simple way.	This activity is more about organising personal data but it can be extended to asking which pets their friends would choose – or taken even further by designing their own survey about pets.	Organising and using data: Sort, classify and organise information in a simple way.	Information handling – Level A/B	AT4 Level 1/2
page 75	Shoes	To organise and present data in a table.	Different kinds of information can be collected in this way using a similar table.	Organising and using data: Sort, classify and organise information in a simple way.	Information handling – Level B	AT4 Level 2
page 76	Free choice	To interpret the results of a survey.	The children could make up their own 'free choice' survey and present the results. They could also extend this survey to other classes.	Organising and using data: Sort, classify and organise information in a simple way.	Information handling – Level B	AT4 Level 2
page 77	Is and is not	To present results of data collection in a table.	A variety of toys could be collected and displayed and the children could use their own criteria. The tables could be used as discussion points for analysing the results.	Organising and using data: Sort, classify and organise information in a simple way.	Information handling – Level B	AT4 Level 2/3

SCHOLASTIC
www.scholastic.co.uk

Page	Activity	Objective	Teachers' notes	National Numeracy Strategy links	Scottish Curriculum links	KS1 Levels
page 78	How likely?	To classify and organise data using given criteria.	It is important to discuss the children's statements. Some statements could fit into more than one pile, according to the children involved.	Organising and using data: Sort, classify and organise information in a simple way.	Information handling – Level B	AT4 Level 2/3
pages 79 and 80	Games and Games graph	To organise data and present it as a simple block graph.	The children may need reminding how to tally. The 'Games' page can be adapted by blanking out the tallies before copying so that the children can survey their own class. Some children may be able to use these pages to devise their own data collection and graph sheets.	Organising and using data: Sort, classify and organise information in a simple way.	Information handling – Level B	AT4 Level 2
page 81	Shape sets	To begin to recognise the properties of similar 2-D shapes.	Children should have had lots of experience of practical sorting before they start this activity, which focuses on the similarities and differences between 2-D shapes.	Shape and space: Use everyday language to recognise and describe features of familiar 2-D shapes.	Shape, position and movement – Level A	AT3 Level 1
page 82	Matching	To begin to recognise the properties of similar 2-D shapes.	This activity is started by matching 'real' shapes with the ones on the page but can be made more difficult as a game with one set of cut-out shapes and one set of written names which have to be matched.	Shape and space: Use everyday language to recognise and describe features of familiar 2-D shapes.	Shape, position and movement – Level A	AT3 Level 1
page 83	Shape jigsaws	To begin to recognise the properties of similar 2-D shapes.	This activity needs to be copied onto thin card. It is a useful activity to have available on a table for children to use again.	Shape and space: Use everyday language to recognise and describe features of familiar 2-D shapes.	Shape, position and movement – Level A	AT3 Level 1
page 84	How many sides?	To begin to recognise the properties of similar 2-D shapes.	The children could be asked to write the names of the common shapes that they recognise, such as triangle, rectangle and square. They could also look at the different appearance of shapes with the same number of sides.	Shape and space: Use everyday language to recognise and describe features of familiar 2-D shapes.	Shape, position and movement – Level A	AT3 Level 1
pages 85 and 86	Shape game – 1 and 2	To begin to recognise the properties of similar 2-D shapes.	The pages need to be copied onto thin card and laminated. Many different games can be played using one of the games or the two games together. They are also useful to take home to play such games as shape snap, pairs or bingo.	Shape and space: Use everyday language to recognise and describe features of familiar 2-D shapes.	Shape, position and movement – Level A	AT3 Level 1
page 87	Building with cubes	To begin to recognise the properties of 3-D shapes.	The children will need sets of linking cubes. They could record their shapes by drawing them, but some children may need help with drawing 3-D shapes.	Shape and space: Make and describe models using everyday 3-D shapes.	Shape, position and movement – Level A	AT3 Level 1
page 88	3-D search	To begin to recognise the properties of 3-D shapes.	This activity could be extended by making a collection of different 3-D shapes or by using the whole school as well as the classroom.	Shape and space: Recognise the features of familiar 3-D shapes.	Shape, position and movement – Level A/B	AT3 Level 1/2
page 89	More matching	To begin to recognise the properties of 3-D shapes.	The children should have many opportunities to talk about and handle 3-D shapes and to begin to recognise 3-D shape names before they do this activity. This page can be copied onto card to make a simple matching game.	Shape and space: Recognise the features of familiar 3-D shapes.	Shape, position and movement – Level A/B	AT3 Level 1/2
page 90	Shape sorting	To sort shapes and describe some of their features using the appropriate vocabulary.	As well as considering the number of sides and corners that a shape has, questions could be asked about whether it can be cut in half – is it symmetrical?	Shape and space: Sort shapes and describe some of their features; begin to recognise lines of symmetry.	Shape, position and movement – Level B	AT3 Level 1/2
page 91	Repeating shapes	To draw repeating and accurate shapes according to a given pattern.	Some children might need templates to draw round to complete the patterns.	Shape and space: Sort shapes and describe some of their features.	Shape, position and movement – Level B	AT3 Level 2

Page	Activity	Objective	Teachers' notes	National Numeracy Strategy links	Scottish Curriculum links	KS1 Levels
page 92	Shipshapes	To match shapes using specific criteria.	Use thin card for the shapes – preferably laminated. Discuss the shapes the children have made. Encourage them to describe the movement of the shapes, considering rotation, translation and reflection. They could also investigate the symmetry of shapes that they have made.	Shape and space: Sort shapes and describe some of their features.	Shape, position and movement – Level B	AT3 Level 2
page 93	Shopping shapes	To look at and identify common 3-D shapes.	You will need to have a good collection of 3-D tins and packaging that represents different shapes. Consider the different ways of sorting the shapes and representing them on diagrams.	Shape and space: Describe and sort solid shapes.	Shape, position and movement – Level B	AT3 Level 2
page 94	3-D structures	To look at and identify common 3-D shapes.	You will need a collection of common 3-D shapes so that the drawings can be matched to them.	Shape and space: Use the mathematical names for common 3-D shapes.	Shape, position and movement – Level B	AT3 Level 2
page 95	The maze	To move through a maze using forward, left and right movements.	Some practical demonstrations in the classroom may be needed. Emphasise that instructions are given as if you are walking in the maze. If possible, enlarge the page so that a stand-up figure can be made to 'walk' through the maze.	Shape and space: Give instructions for moving along a route in straight lines.	Shape, position and movement – Level B	AT3 Level 2
page 96	Finding the way	To describe direction and routes.	Remind the children which side is left and which is right. The grid could be adapted by adding more people or buildings, or by enlarging it and using objects and figures.	Shape and space: Give instructions for moving along a route in straight lines.	Shape, position and movement – Level B	AT3 Level 2
page 97	Caterpillars	To compare length and begin to use the vocabulary of length.	This activity can be introduced by asking the children to compare lengths of ribbons or strips of paper. Encourage the children to use vocabulary such as long, short, longest, shorter, and so on.	Measures: Compare lengths by direct comparison.	Number, money and measurement – Level A	AT3 Level 1
page 98	As long as	To compare length and begin to use the vocabulary of length.	Don't forget to allow the children to complete the practical activities using Plasticine and/or linking cubes. Adapt this activity by looking at the term 'as tall as'.	Measures: Compare lengths by direct comparison.	Number, money and measurement – Level A	AT3 Level 1
page 99	Aliens	To compare height and begin to use the vocabulary of: tall, taller, tallest; short, shorter, shortest.	Ask the children to put groups of their friends in order from tallest to shortest.	Measures: Compare lengths by direct comparison.	Number, money and measurement – Level A	AT3 Level 1
page 100	Smaller than your hand	To begin to develop the idea of non-standard measurements.	The children should be encouraged to compare real classroom objects with their hands.	Measures: Measure length using non-standard units.	Number, money and measurement – Level A	AT3 Level 1
page 101	What shall I use?	To begin to make decisions about non-standard units.	Some practice of using non-standard measures will be useful before starting this activity.	Measures: Suggest suitable non-standard units for measuring length.	Number, money and measurement – Level A/B	AT3 Level 1/2
page 102	Measuring with hands and feet	To begin to make decisions about non-standard units.	The children could make a 'measure' from a strip of paper using an appropriate body part – hand span, index finger, foot length, and so on. Explain that early units of measurement were based on parts of the human body. For example, a 'palm' was the width of four fingers, and in the UK and US horses' heights are still measured in 'hands' which is based on the breadth of a male human hand, which is about 10cm. However, these types of units are not always accurate as people differ in size.	Measures: Suggest suitable non-standard units for measuring length.	Number, money and measurement – Level B	AT3 Level 2

SCHOLASTIC
www.scholastic.co.uk

Page	Activity	Objective	Teachers' notes	National Numeracy Strategy links	Scottish Curriculum links	KS1 Levels
page 103	Weigh the apple	To compare mass by direct comparison.	The children will need access to bucket balances, apples, and a wide range of objects that may or may not balance the apple.	Measures: Suggest suitable non-standard units for measuring mass.	Number, money and measurement – Level A	AT3 Level 1
page 104	Using a balance	To compare mass by direct comparison and begin to use the vocabulary of heavier and lighter.	A wide range of objects that are easy to handle by the children will be needed.	Measures: Suggest suitable non-standard units for measuring mass.	Number, money and measurement – Level A/B	AT3 Level 1/2
page 105	Blocks	To compare mass by direct comparison and begin to use the vocabulary of heavier and lighter.	The blocks are used as non-standard units of measurement. Encourage the children to estimate before completing this activity. Emphasise that an estimate does not have to be accurate, but the children should consider the 'reasonableness' of answers.	Measures: Use uniform non-standard units to measure mass.	Number, money and measurement – Level A/B	AT3 Level 1/2
page 106	My shoe	To compare mass by direct comparison and begin to use the vocabulary of heavier and lighter.	A wide range of objects will be needed. The children should know that they do not need to balance items one for one, and they can balance several items of one object to balance the shoe.	Measures: Use uniform non-standard units to measure mass.	Number, money and measurement – Level A	AT3 Level 1
page 107	Bottles	To compare capacity by direct comparison.	Each child or group will need three bottles, a yoghurt pot and a bowl of water. They may need to be taught how to use funnels.	Measures: Use uniform non-standard units to measure capacity.	Number, money and measurement – Level A	AT3 Level 1
page 108	Sand	To compare capacity by direct comparison.	The sand will have to be perfectly dry in order to pour easily. The children could record their results by drawing spoons, or by using a tally or a frequency table.	Measures: Use uniform non-standard units to measure capacity.	Number, money and measurement – Level A	AT3 Level 1
page 109	Night and day	To begin to look at familiar events related to time.	This could be extended and the children encouraged to make up their own set of cards of what they do at night and in the daytime.	Measures: Order familiar events in time and use the vocabulary related to time.	Number, money and measurement – Level A	AT3 Level 1/2
page 110	O'clock	To match time to the hour.	The copies of the game would be better laminated on thin card. The children need to be able to tell the time in whole hours, and it may be helpful to practise with real clocks.	Measures: Read the time to the hour.	Number, money and measurement – Level A/B	AT3 Level 1/2
page 111	The seasons	To match activities with seasons of the year.	There should be a lot of discussion about the seasons before this activity is completed. Some children will be able to write down the months of the year in each column.	Measures: Know the seasons of the year.	Number, money and measurement – Level A/B	AT3 Level 1/2
page 112	Paperclips	To measure items using a non-standard unit.	Check that each child does use ten paperclips. This means it is possible to compare results for accuracy. The children could use other units of non-standard measurements, such as straws on a string or linking cubes.	Measures: Use the vocabulary related to length.	Number, money and measurement – Level B	AT3 Level 2
page 113	A metre	To measure objects using a metre as a standard unit.	This activity introduces a metre as a standard unit of measurement. Compare results for accuracy.	Measures: Measure lengths using standard units.	Number, money and measurement – Level B	AT3 Level 2/3
page 114	Snails	To measure lines in centimetres.	This activity asks the children to measure distances which are not single straight lines. Compare results for accuracy. Answers: 1st Bill, 2nd Paul, 3rd John, 4th Boris.	Measures: Measure lengths using standard units.	Number, money and measurement – Level B	AT3 Level 2/3
page 115	Make a metre	To use a metre stick as a scale and measure and compare lengths.	Children will need help converting dice. This game can be adapted for any length.	Measures: Read a simple scale and use the standard unit of a metre.	Number, money and measurement – Level B	AT3 Level 2/3

Page	Activity	Objective	Teachers' notes	National Numeracy Strategy links	Scottish Curriculum links	KS1 Levels
page 116	The estimating game	To estimate and measure in metres and centimetres.	Check how accurately the children are measuring in metres and centimetres, and ensure that they are clear which objects are being measured. The cards can be laminated and the children can introduce their own cards.	Measures: Record estimates and measurements.	Number, money and measurement – Level B	AT3 Level 2
page 117	Changing shape	To weigh objects using non-standard measures.	Emphasise to the children that they must use the same lump of Plasticine each time – it is only the shape that changes. This activity demonstrates the conservation of mass.	Measures: Begin to use the vocabulary related to mass.	Number, money and measurement – Level B	AT3 Level 2
page 118	Kilograms	To balance various objects against one kilogram.	Remember to tell the children to take care with plastic bags. Discuss with the children how they made their ½kg bags of sand and compare their methods.	Measures: Measure and compare mass using standard units.	Number, money and measurement – Level B	AT3 Level 2
page 119	Predicting	To predict and measure mass in standard units.	The children will need to recognise weights in grams and will need help in arriving at accurate results. Emphasise that a level cup is needed for a fair test.	Measures: Measure and compare mass using standard units.	Number, money and measurement – Level B	AT3 Level 2/3
page 120	Grams	To predict and measure mass in standard units.	Remind the children to estimate the weight first each time. There needs to be a good collection of small objects to weigh. Make sure they understand that 1000g are in 1kg.	Measures: Measure and compare mass using standard units.	Number, money and measurement – Level B	AT3 Level 2/3
page 121	Full or empty?	To begin to use vocabulary associated with capacity.	Children may need to look at some actual classroom containers for examples of what 'full' or 'empty' means.	Measures: Estimate and measure capacity using non-standard units.	Number, money and measurement – Level B	AT3 Level 2
page 122	Half-full	To begin to use vocabulary associated with capacity.	Children may need to look at some actual classroom containers for examples of what 'full' or 'empty' means. Younger or less able children may only realise that a container is neither full nor empty, with no concept of the fractions in between. Older or more able children may realise that 'half-full' and 'half empty' mean the same thing.	Measures: Estimate and measure capacity using non-standard units.	Number, money and measurement – Level B	AT3 Level 2
page 123	Which holds most?	To begin to use vocabulary associated with capacity.	You will need to select containers with different capacities for this activity. The children can either use sand or water for pouring. They will have to ensure a container is full before pouring its contents into the next one.	Measures: Estimate and measure capacity using non-standard units.	Number, money and measurement – Level B	AT3 Level 2
page 124	Litres	To use the vocabulary for capacity and understand how much a litre is.	You will need to select containers with different capacities for this activity. This activity explores a litre as a standard unit of measurement. Fill each of the smaller containers and then pour the contents into the litre measure to find its capacity.	Measures: Measure capacity using standard units.	Number, money and measurement – Level B	AT3 Level 2
page 125	Make a litre	To use the vocabulary for capacity and understand how much a litre is.	You will need to select containers with different capacities for this activity. This activity explores the actual quantity of liquid needed to make a litre. The children can develop their estimation skills relating to litres.	Measures: Measure capacity using standard units.	Number, money and measurement – Level B	AT3 Level 2
page 126	In a minute	To use a specific unit of time.	The children need to understand what a minute 'feels like' as a length of time. They could devise other ways of calculating a minute.	Measures: Use units of time and know the relationships between them.	Number, money and measurement – Level B	AT3 Level 2
page 127	Seconds	To use a specific unit of time.	The children should be able to operate a stopwatch accurately. Remind the children that the watch must be reset for each activity.	Measures: Use units of time and know the relationships between them.	Number, money and measurement – Level B	AT3 Level 2/3

■SCHOLASTIC
www.scholastic.co.uk

Bags of apples

✤ Count how many apples in each bag. Put the correct number on each label.

✤ Cut out the numbers below and put them in order, from smallest to largest.
✤ Put the correct number of buttons or cubes with each one.

9 1 7 4 0 6 2 5 8 3

Sets

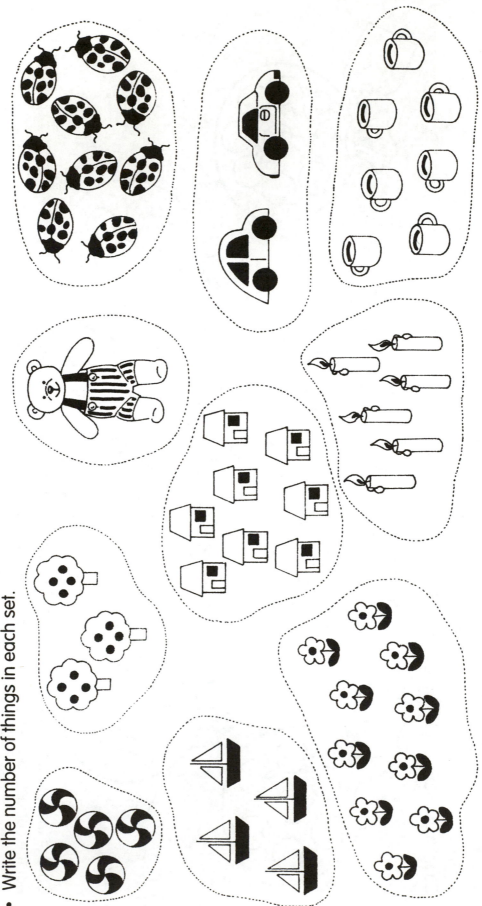

❖ Cut out the sets. Count how many things there are in each set.

❖ Stick them in your book, starting with a set of one and ending with a set of ten.

❖ Write the number of things in each set.

❖ Make some sets for yourself.

■SCHOLASTIC
www.scholastic.co.uk

Name _____

Peanuts

◆ Colour in the peanuts. How many peanuts has each parrot got?

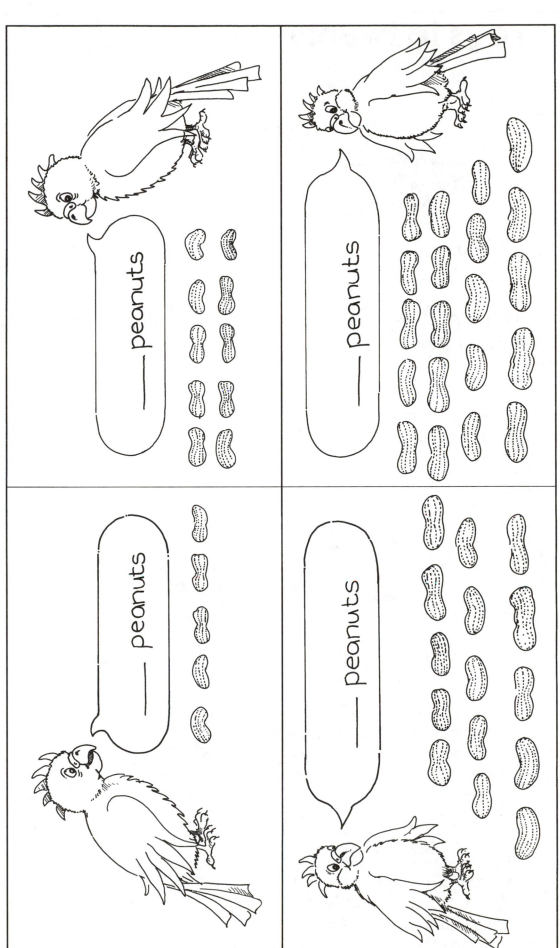

___ peanuts

___ peanuts

___ peanuts

___ peanuts

Legs to twenty

How to play:

Here is one way to play with these cards. Perhaps you could make up some other games, too?

1. Shuffle the cards.
Spread them all out separately, face down.

2. Turn over any four cards.

How many legs have you got?

I've got none, four, four and six... that's 14!

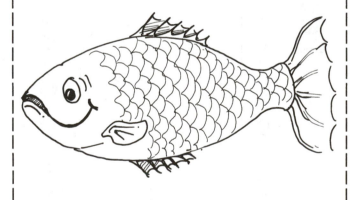

3. If you've got <u>less</u> than 20 legs, you keep the cards. If you've got <u>more</u> than 20 legs, turn the cards back again.

If you get <u>exactly</u> 20 legs you keep the cards and that's the end of the game.

4. Now it's your friend's turn.
Who can get the most cards?

SCHOLASTIC
www.scholastic.co.uk

Name _____

SCHOLASTIC
www.scholastic.co.uk

Missing numbers

Fill in the missing numbers.

0, 1, 2, 3, ☐, 5, 6, ☐, 8, 9

5, 6, ☐, 8, 9, ☐, 11, 12

8, 7, ☐, 5, 4, 3, ☐, 1, ☐

7, 6, ☐, 4, ☐, 2, ☐, 0

10, ☐, 8, ☐, 6, 5, ☐, 3

Three in a line

Find the numbers in between.

9 | | 7

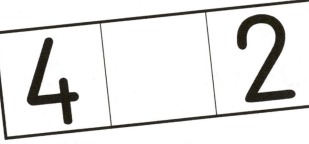

4 | | 2

3 | | 1

10 | | 8

7 | | 9

0 | | 2   4 | | 6

Telephones

Fill in the missing numbers.

Colouring numbers

Colour in all the even numbers.

1	2	3	4
5	6	7	8
9	10	11	12
13	14	15	16
17	18	19	20

1	2
3	4
5	6
7	8
9	10
11	12
13	14
15	16
17	18
19	20

1	2	3	4	5
6	7	8	9	10
11	12	13	14	15
16	17	18	19	20

Look at the patterns you have made.

Dice patterns

The spots on a dice usually have a special pattern for each number.

Draw the patterns here.

| 1 | 2 | 3 | 4 | 5 | 6 |

If 1 is on the top what number is on the bottom?

_____

If 3 is on the top what number is on the bottom?

_____

If 5 is on the top what number is on the bottom?

_____

Snakes and ladders

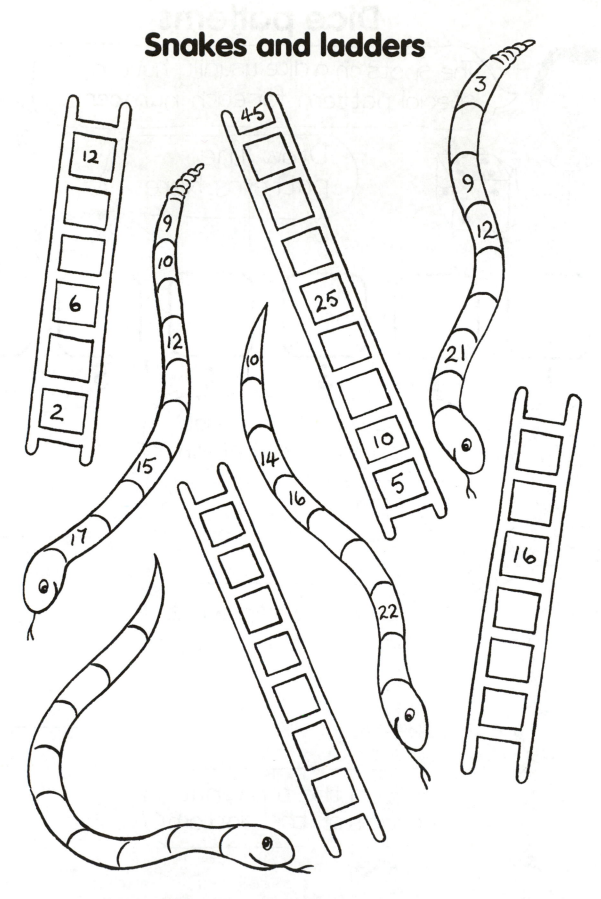

✤ Complete these number sequences and then make up some of your own.

SCHOLASTIC
www.scholastic.co.uk

Name _____

The puzzled postie

Can you help the new postie deliver his letters? He will walk along one side of the road and then back along the other side.

♣ Write the numbers on the houses.

♣ Sort the letters into odd and even numbers and then draw his delivery route.

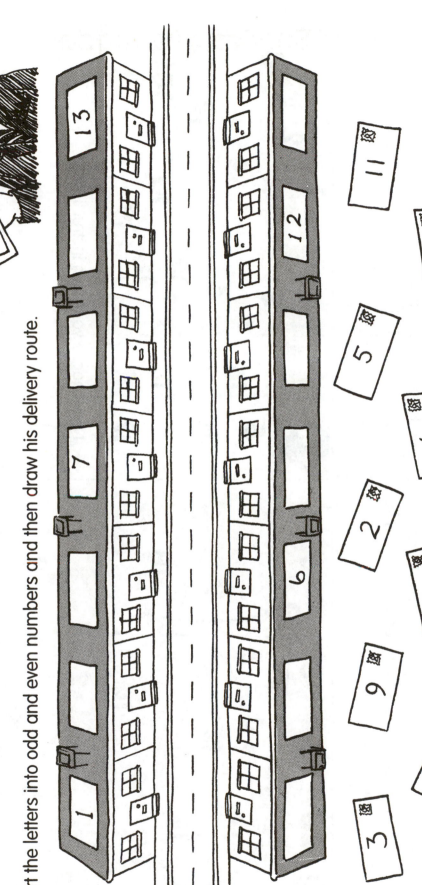

A-r-r-o-w-g-r-a-p-h-s

♣ How many chains of numbers can you find in each arrowgraph by following the instruction given in the top left-hand corner? Use a different colour for each chain. One has been done to start you off.

+3

20 2 3 6

10

1 13 9 8

5 4 7 18

17 12 11

16 14 7

15

19

+4

5 16 4 1

13 3 12 2

7 6 9

15

17 11 20 14

19

18

×2

2 6 3 7

1 5 9 8 14

4 12 13 16 15

10 11 18 17

20 19

✱ Now choose your own instruction.

○

1 2 7 3 13 5 4

8 11 6 12 15

9 10 17 16

18 19 20 14

19

SCHOLASTIC
www.scholastic.co.uk

57	45	89
69	94	23
70	38	17

Number cards 3

* Cut out the number cards and put them in order from the lowest to the highest.
* Write any number from 0 to 99 on the blank cards and put them into the correct place in the lowest to highest order.
* On the back of each card, draw an abacus picture to match the number. One has been done for you.

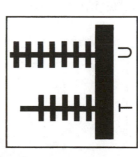

57

Can you think of a game to play with a friend, using these cards?

Three-digit numbers

✤ What three-digit numbers can you make using these numerals? You may only use each numeral once in each number. Write the numbers in order from the smallest to the largest.

✤ Which number contains most hundreds?
✤ Which number has the largest number in the tens column?
✤ Which number has the largest number in the units column?

✤ Try again, using the following numerals.

NO FUSS
PHOTOCOPIABLE

SCHOLASTIC
www.scholastic.co.uk

Name _____

Number spiral

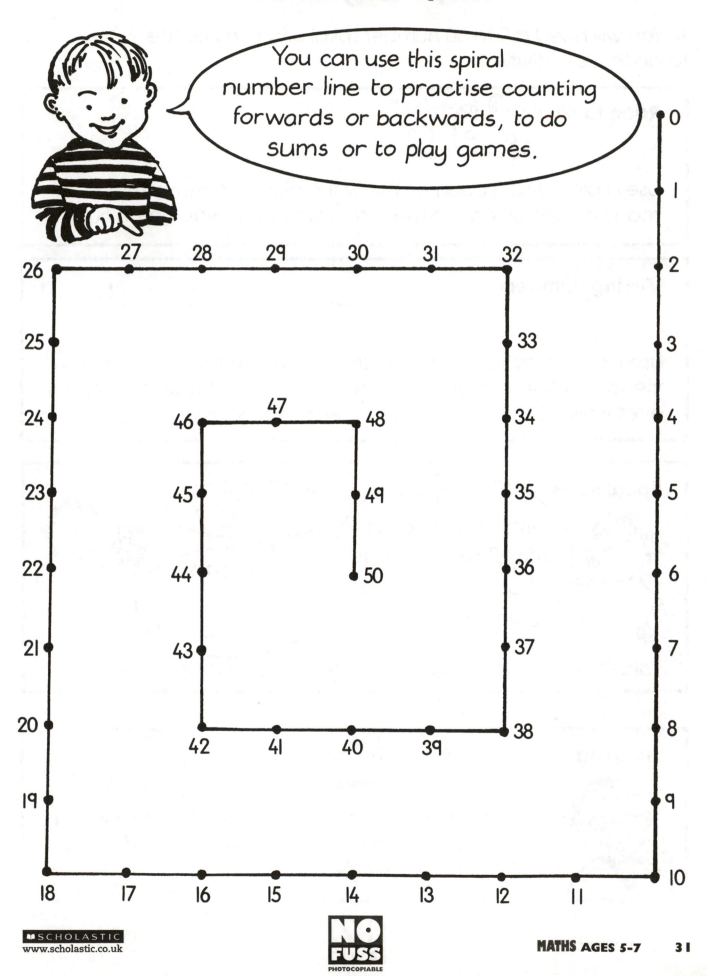

You can use this spiral number line to practise counting forwards or backwards, to do sums or to play games.

Spiral games

◆ You will need a 0 to 50 number spiral or a number line to do these activities.

Race to 50

Use a dice and a counter. Throw the dice and move that many places along the line. How quickly can you get to 50?

Missing numbers

Use six counters to cover over six numbers on the spiral. Ask your friend to tell you what the missing numbers are! Then shut your eyes while your friend covers some numbers for you to guess.

Spiral sums

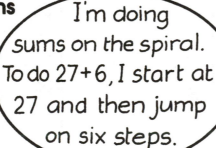

I'm doing sums on the spiral. To do 27 + 6, I start at 27 and then jump on six steps.

Did you get 33?

You can check with a calculator.

Take it in turns with a friend, to make up sums for each other.

Jumping

Start at 0. Jump three places at a time. You will land on 3, then 6, then 9, then..?

Can you get exactly to 50? What happens if you jump five each time?

SCHOLASTIC
www.scholastic.co.uk

Name _____

Halves

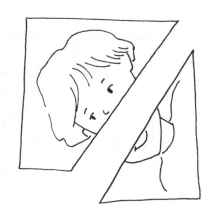

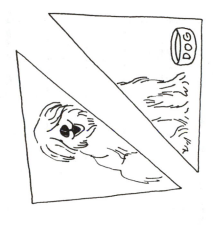

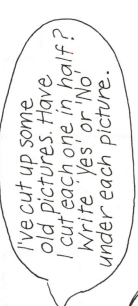

I've cut up some old pictures. Have I cut each one in half? Write 'Yes' or 'No' under each picture.

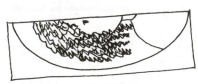

Halves

* Make tracings of the shapes below and keep them safely on one side.
* Cut out the shapes on this paper. Cut each shape in half. Colour each half a different colour.

* When you have cut and coloured each shape, fit them back onto your traced shapes.

Name _____

Dominoes

❖ Look at a set of dominoes. Find a domino which has 8 spots on it altogether.

❖ Find all the dominoes which have a total of 8 spots on them. Draw these dominoes here.

❖ Make these dominoes have a total of 6 spots. Each one should be different.

❖ Can you find any dominoes in the set like the ones you have made?

❖ Are there any that are different to the ones that you have made?

Name _____

Crabs – 1

There are 5 crabs in each picture but some have crawled under the seaweed.

How many are hiding? ☐

How many are hiding? ☐

How many are hiding? ☐

Name _____

Crabs – 2

There are 5 crabs in each picture but some have crawled under the seaweed.

  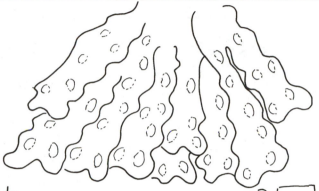

How many are hiding ? □

How many are hiding ? □

How many are hiding ? □

Name _____

Hedgehogs – 1

There are 8 hedgehogs in each picture but some are still asleep under the leaves. How many are asleep?

 +  = 8

___ are asleep.

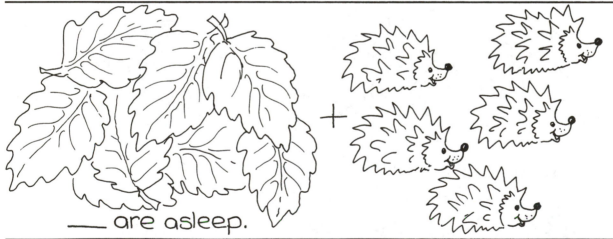 = 8

___ are asleep.

 +  = 8

___ are asleep.

SCHOLASTIC
www.scholastic.co.uk

Name _____

Hedgehogs – 2

Colour in and cut out the hedgehogs and piles of leaves. Now use them to make some sums that make 8.

NO FUSS PHOTOCOPIABLE

Number 10

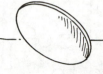
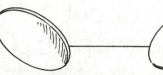

Fill in the spaces and look at the pattern.

$10 + \boxed{} = 10$

$9 + \boxed{} = 10$

$8 + \boxed{} = 10$

$7 + \boxed{} = 10$

$6 + \boxed{} = 10$

$5 + \boxed{} = 10$

$4 + \boxed{} = 10$

$3 + \boxed{} = 10$

$2 + \boxed{} = 10$

$1 + \boxed{} = 10$

$0 + \boxed{} = 10$

Use 10 counters to help you.

NO FUSS PHOTOCOPIABLE

SCHOLASTIC
www.scholastic.co.uk

Name _____

Up and downstairs

◆ Draw some people on each bus.

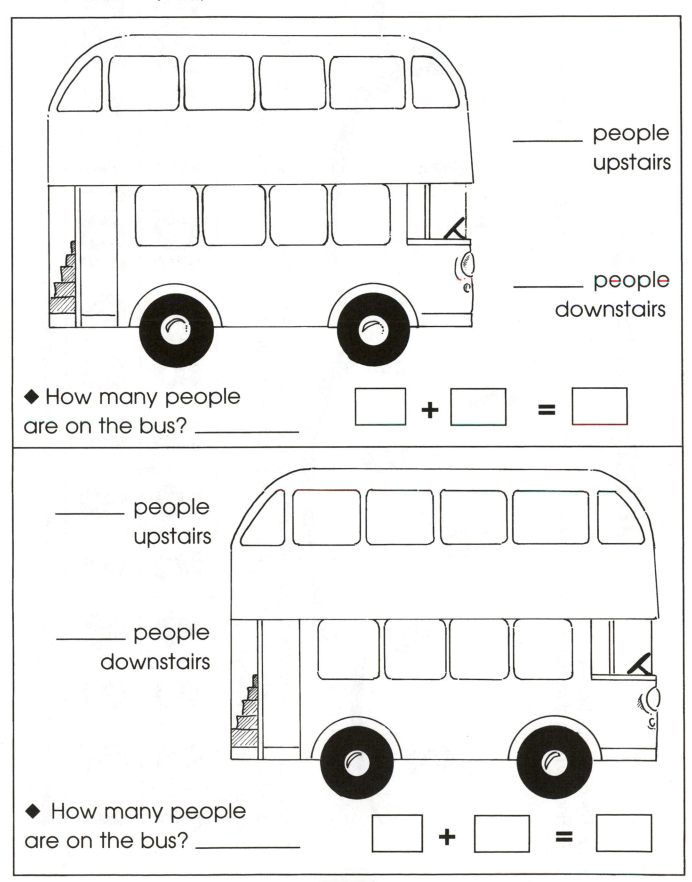

_____ people upstairs

_____ people downstairs

◆ How many people are on the bus? _____

☐ + ☐ = ☐

_____ people upstairs

_____ people downstairs

◆ How many people are on the bus? _____

☐ + ☐ = ☐

NO FUSS
PHOTOCOPIABLE

Name _____

Difference pairs 4 6 12

9 6 3

❖ The difference between 3 and 7 is 4.
❖ Find the pairs of numbers where the difference between them is 4. Join the pair together by drawing a line.

2

5

7

4

6

9

3

8

❖ You could use the number tracks below to help you. To check that the difference between 3 and 7 is 4, put 3 buttons or counters on one number line and 7 buttons or counters on the other. Count that the difference between them is 4.

1	2	3	4	5	6	7	8	9	10	11	12	13	14
1	2	3	4	5	6	7	8	9	10	11	12	13	14

❖ Write some more pairs of numbers where the difference between them is 4.

Name _____

❧ What do you have to add to help the frog jump from one lily-pad to the next?

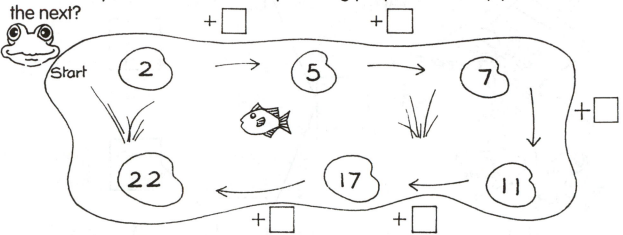

❧ Write down what you have done in the following way:

$2 + \square = 5$ $5 + \square = 7$ $7 + \square = 11$

$11 + \square = 17$ $17 + \square = 22$

❧ Make your own jumping frog activity.

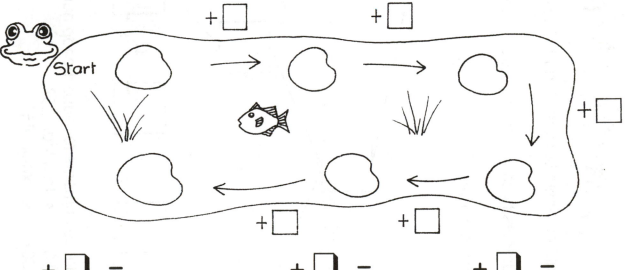

$\_ + \square = \_$ $\_ + \square = \_$ $\_ + \square = \_$

$\_ + \square = \_$ $\_ + \square = \_$

❧ Try the same activity using subtraction instead of addition.

NO FUSS PHOTOCOPIABLE

Name _____

Pyram-adds

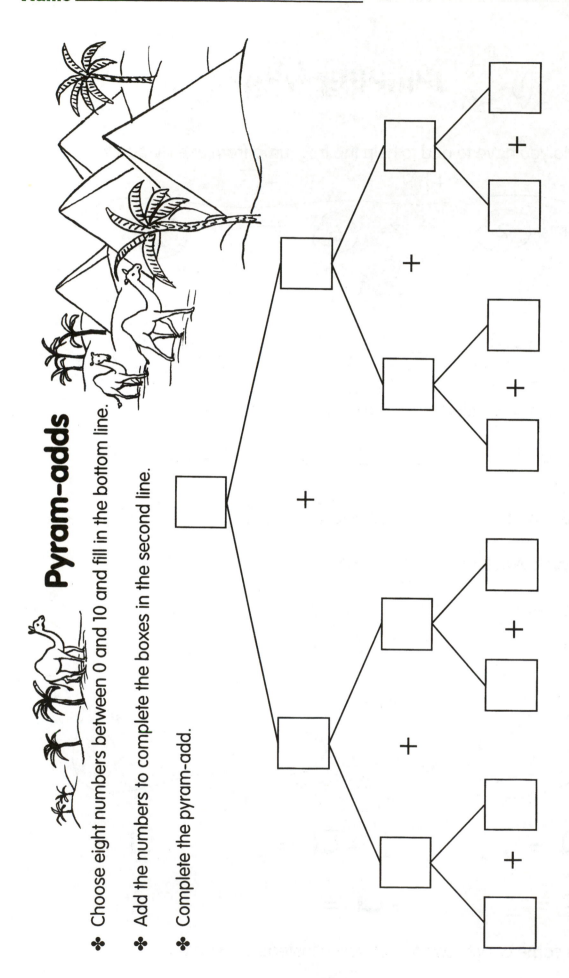

✢ Choose eight numbers between 0 and 10 and fill in the bottom line.

✢ Add the numbers to complete the boxes in the second line.

✢ Complete the pyram-add.

✢ Can you choose numbers to make the top number:
- more than 50? • less than 25?
- more than 80? • exactly 46?

NO FUSS
PHOTOCOPIABLE

Name _____

Reducing squares

This is a reducing square. Whatever numbers you start with, they reduce to 0.

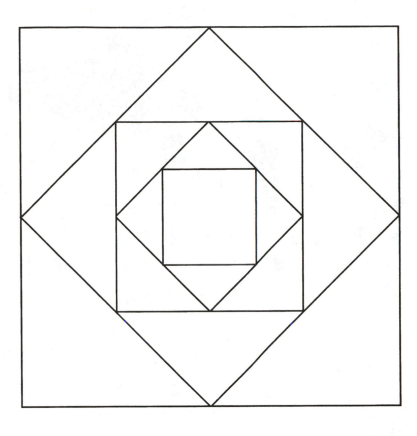

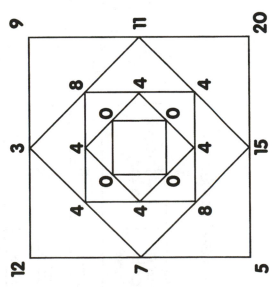

✤ Investigate some reducing squares of your own.
● Put any four numbers at the corners of the outer square opposite.
● Work out the difference between each pair of corner numbers to get the corner number of the next square.
● Find the next four corners in the same way.
● Continue doing this until you get to 0. Add more squares if you need to.

✤ Try using different sets of corner numbers. Do you notice any patterns?

Name _____

Buns for bears

✿ Can you share the buns in the basket so that each bear has the same number?

✿✿ Are there any left over?

✿✿ If you had 16 buns how many would each bear have?

✿ Complete this table:

If each bear is to have	I will need to buy
2 buns	8
3 buns	12
4 buns	
5 buns	
6 buns	
7 buns	
8 buns	

■SCHOLASTIC
www.scholastic.co.uk

Name _____

Marbles

I'll score 4 points for each marble I roll which stops on the star.

◆ How many points did I score?

Make up some 'Marble' questions for your friends.

Bus sums 1

How many people are on these buses?
Use counters to help you, if you want.

10 upstairs
4 downstairs

| 10 | + | 4 | = | |

6 upstairs
3 downstairs

| | + | | = | |

7 upstairs
8 downstairs

| | + | | = | |

11 upstairs
3 downstairs

| | + | | = | |

5 upstairs
7 downstairs

| | + | | = | |

Does it matter if you count upstairs or downstairs first?

NO FUSS PHOTOCOPIABLE

Name _____

Bus sums 2

These sums are for

_____

Make up some sums. Give them to your friend to try.

Tins

Do you like baked beans or sweetcorn the best?

◆ Colour them in.

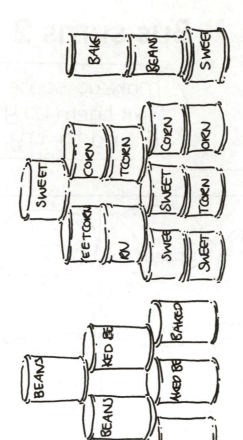

How many tins of beans are there? _____

How many tins of sweetcorn? _____

How many tins altogether? _____

Fruit

Do you like apples or bananas the best?

◆ Colour them in.

How many apples are there? _____

How many bananas are there? _____

How many pieces of fruit altogether? _____

Seeds

◆ Give each parrot _____ sunflower seeds.

How many seeds altogether?

$\boxed{} + \boxed{} + \boxed{} + \boxed{} = \boxed{}$

$4 \times \boxed{} = \boxed{}$

Seed sums

I found 14 seeds,
then I ate 4 of them.

How many
seeds are left? _____

Check with a calculator.

I found 20 seeds,
then I ate 7 of them.

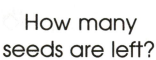

How many
seeds are left? _____

Check with a calculator.

Make up your own sum.

I found ___ seeds,
then I ate ___ of them.

How many
seeds are left? _____

Check with a calculator.

Number routes

✿ Follow the arrows along each route from 'start' to 'finish' and add the numbers.

✿ Can you find a route that gives a total of 14?

✿ Which route gives the highest total?

✿ Which route gives the lowest total?

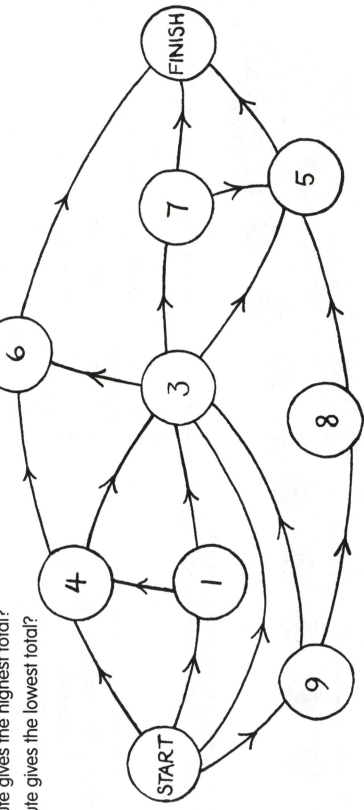

✿ What happens if you change some of the arrows?
Investigate some different routes.

✿ Draw your own number routes. Try them on a friend.

Name _____

Travelling by train

❖ How many people can you see on the train?

❖ Draw two people in each of the empty carriages.

❖ Fill in this table:

Carriages	Total number of people
1	2
2	4
3	
4	
5	

❖ How many people do you think there would be in:

Number of carriages	Guess	Check
10 carriages		
20 carriages		
50 carriages		
100 carriages		

❖ Use a calculator – but guess first!

SCHOLASTIC
www.scholastic.co.uk

Bull's-eye

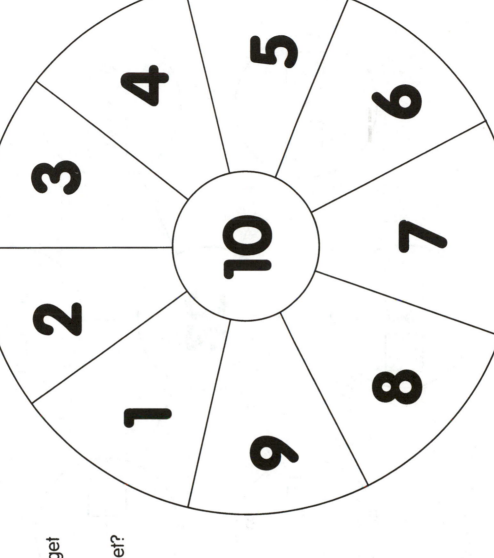

You have three darts.
Each dart must score.

♣ What is the highest score you can get
on this dartboard?

♣ What is the lowest score you can get?

♣ If only one
dart can land in each number:

• what is the highest score?

• what is the lowest score?

Name _____

Some sums

÷ × + − + × ÷

♣ Fill in the sums below to give the answer 20. One is done for you.

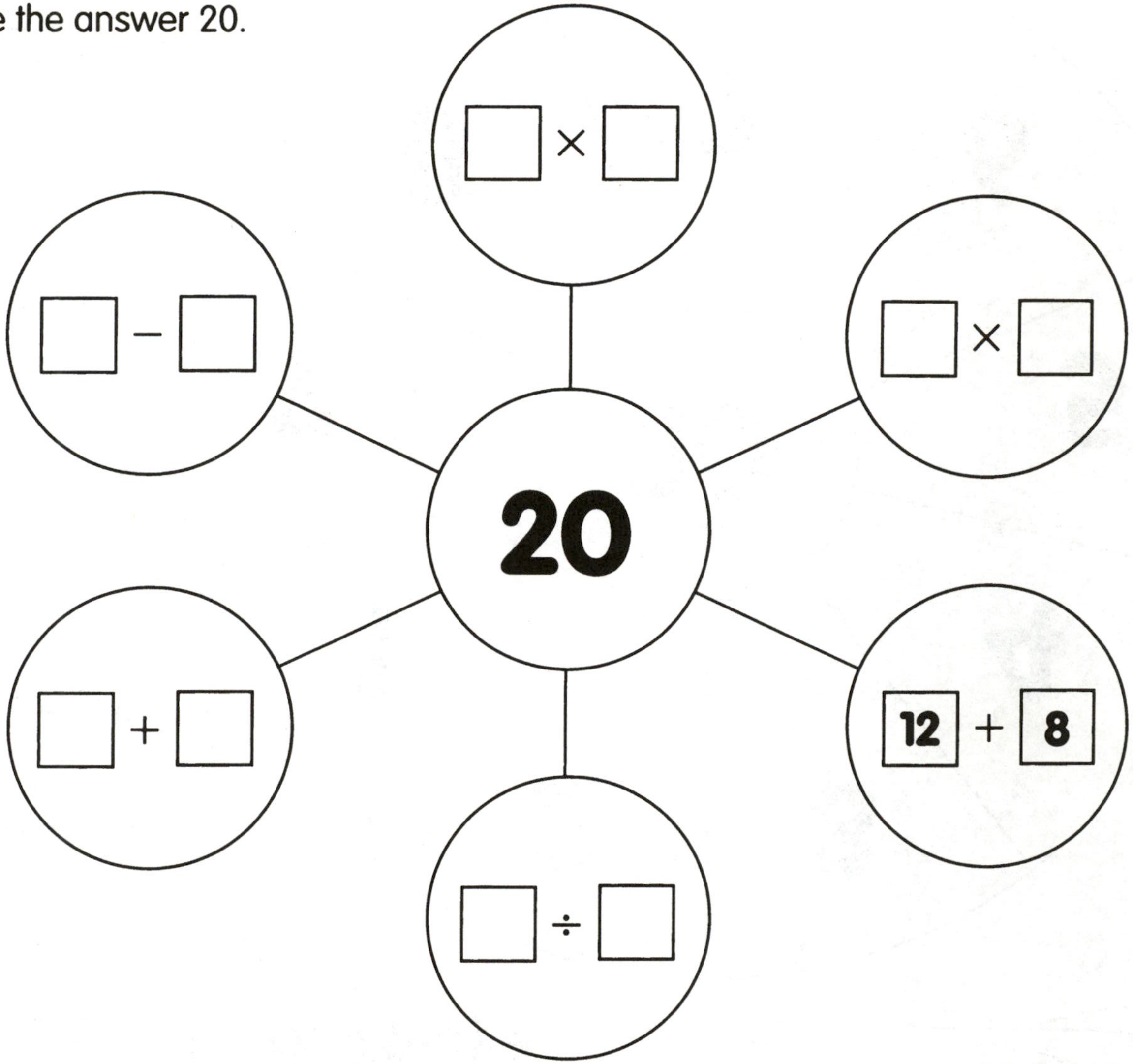

Central circle: **20**, connected to circles containing:
- □ × □
- 12 + 8
- □ ÷ □
- □ + □
- □ − □
- □ × □

♣ Are there any more ways of making 20?

♣ Investigate how many ways you can make:
- + sums;
- − sums;
- × sums;
- ÷ sums.

Magic squares

Magic squares were devised by the Chinese thousands of years ago. In a magic square each line adds up to the same total.

♣ Complete this magic square opposite.

The magic square total is 18.

5	10	
	6	
		7

♣ Now multiply each of the original numbers by 2. Is it still a magic square?

Will this work for any nine consecutive numbers?

What about negative numbers?

♣ Complete these magic squares.

-2	3	2
	1	
		4

10	35	
	25	
		40

♣ Take the same numbers as above and add 12 to each of them.

♣ Is it still a magic square?

Make 57

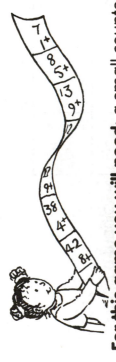

7	2	5
3	1	8
6	9	4

For this game you will need: a small counter, a pencil, paper and a partner.

♣ The object of the game is to make exactly 57 or force your partner to make more than 57.

● Put the counter on any number and write the number down on the paper.

● Get your partner to move the counter to any square NOT in the same row or column. For example, with the counter on 6 your partner cannot move it to 3, 7, 9 or 4.

● Add this new number to the first number.

● Play continues in turns, adding each number to the previous one.

● The winner is the player to make a total of 57 or to force the other player to get more than 57.

◼SCHOLASTIC
www.scholastic.co.uk

Name _____

The ten pence game

◆ Use the instructions printed below, with the playing cards printed on page 60, to make this game.

A more difficult, but similar, game is on pages 67 and 68.

1 Shuffle the cards.
Put them in a pile, face down, in the middle.

2 Take it in turns to take a card from the top of the pile.
Put it face up, in front of you.

3 Add up how much money you've got as you go along.

4 If you reach exactly 10p, call out, 'TEN PENCE!'
You have won!

If you get <u>more</u> than 10p, call out 'BUST' and drop out
of the game.

'The ten pence game' playing cards

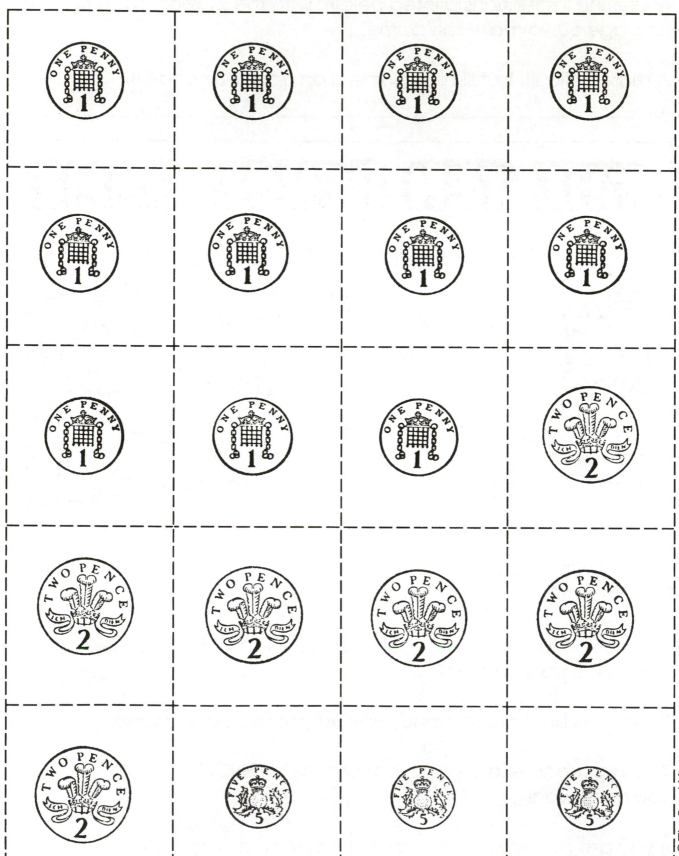

NO FUSS
PHOTOCOPIABLE

■ SCHOLASTIC
www.scholastic.co.uk

Coins © The Royal Mint

Nam_____

Jumble toys

I went to a jumble sale.
Here's what I bought.

I paid with a 20p.

How much change did I get?

I paid with a 20p.

How much change did I get?

I paid with a 50p.

How much change did I get?

If ▢ = 5p
⬚ = 2p
⬚ = 1p

How much are these stacks
of cubes worth?

① ▢ =

② ▢ =

Money track

* You need: 10 1p coins, 11 2p coins, a die and a sand-timer.
* Place the coins on the track as shown. Set the sand-timer.
* Start at START.
* Throw the die. Count on that number around the track. Pick up the coin that you land on. Keep going around until the sand-timer runs out. How much have you collected?
* Put the coins back on the track. Have another try. Do you think you will collect more, less or the same amount this time?

START

Name _____

Classroom shop

✿ Here are some of the things in the class shop.

✿ Use 1p coins. Give each of the children below 10p. Will each child have enough money to buy all of the things on their list?

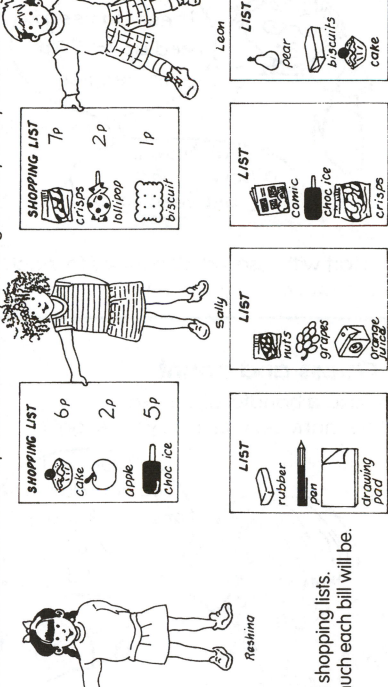

SHOPPING LIST
apple 2p
choc ice 5p
chocolate bar 3p

Reshma

SHOPPING LIST
cake 6p
apple 2p
choc ice 5p

Sally

SHOPPING LIST
crisps 7p
lollipop 2p
biscuit 1p

Leon

LIST
rubber
pen
drawing pad

LIST
nuts
grapes
orange juice

LIST
comic
choc ice
crisps

LIST
pear
biscuits
cake

✿ Put prices on these shopping lists. Then work out how much each bill will be.

NO FUSS
PHOTOCOPIABLE

Name _____

Penny games

To play these games, you need up to 50p in pennies.

Put them in a bowl or box between you.

Take turns to play. Check each other's counting.

◆ To start with, use just 30 pennies for each activity.
Then use 40, then try with 50.

1 Guess and count
◆ Take a handful of pennies.
How many do you think you've got?

Count and see how close you are. Can you get better at guessing?

NO FUSS PHOTOCOPIABLE

SCHOLASTIC
www.scholastic.co.uk

2 What's left?

◆ Take a handful of pennies.
Count how many you've got.

We're using 40 pennies.
I've got 26 !

Can you work out how many are left in the bowl without counting them ?

3 Groups

◆ Choose a number: 2, 3, 4, 5 or 6.
Suppose you chose 4. Put the pennies in groups of 4.

I'm using 30 pennies.

How many groups can you make ?

How many pennies are left over ?

◆ Take it in turns to choose how many pennies to start with.
◆ Can you work out, in your head, how many groups you will make? Check with the pennies.

Bus fares

How could you give each bus driver exactly the right money?

Name _____

The fifty pence game

◆ Use the rules printed below, with the playing cards printed on page 68, to make this game.

An easier version of the game is on pages 59 and 60.

 -

1 Shuffle the cards.
Put them in a pile, face down, in the middle.

2 Take it in turns to take a card from the top of the pile.
Put your cards face up, in front of you.

3 Add up how much money you've got as you go along.

4 If you reach exactly 50p, call out, 'FIFTY PENCE!'
You have won!

If you get <u>more</u> than 50p, call out 'BUST' and drop out
of the game.

NO FUSS
PHOTOCOPIABLE

'The fifty pence game' playing cards

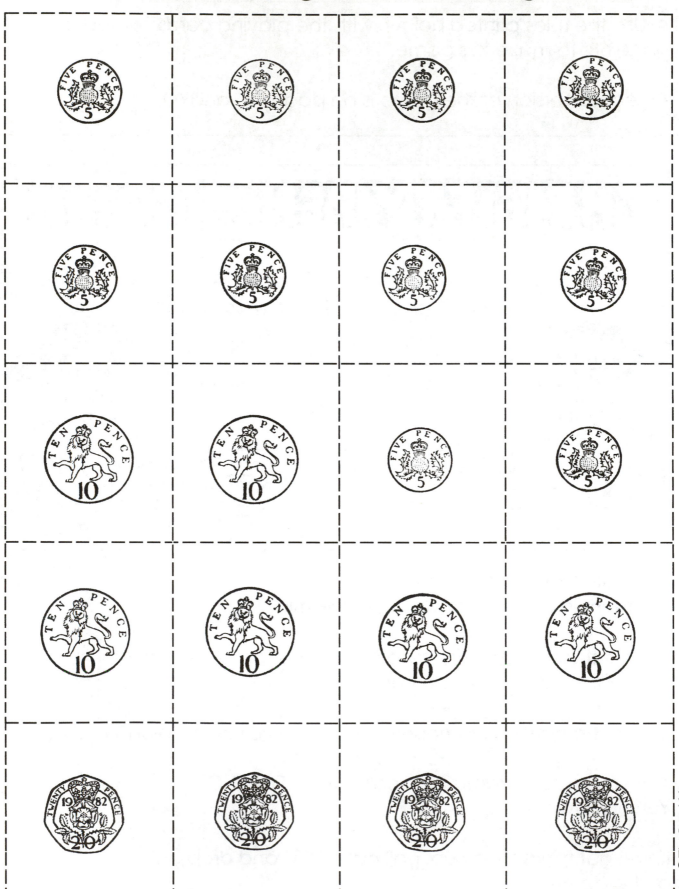

NO FUSS
PHOTOCOPIABLE

Name _____

Coins © The Royal Mint

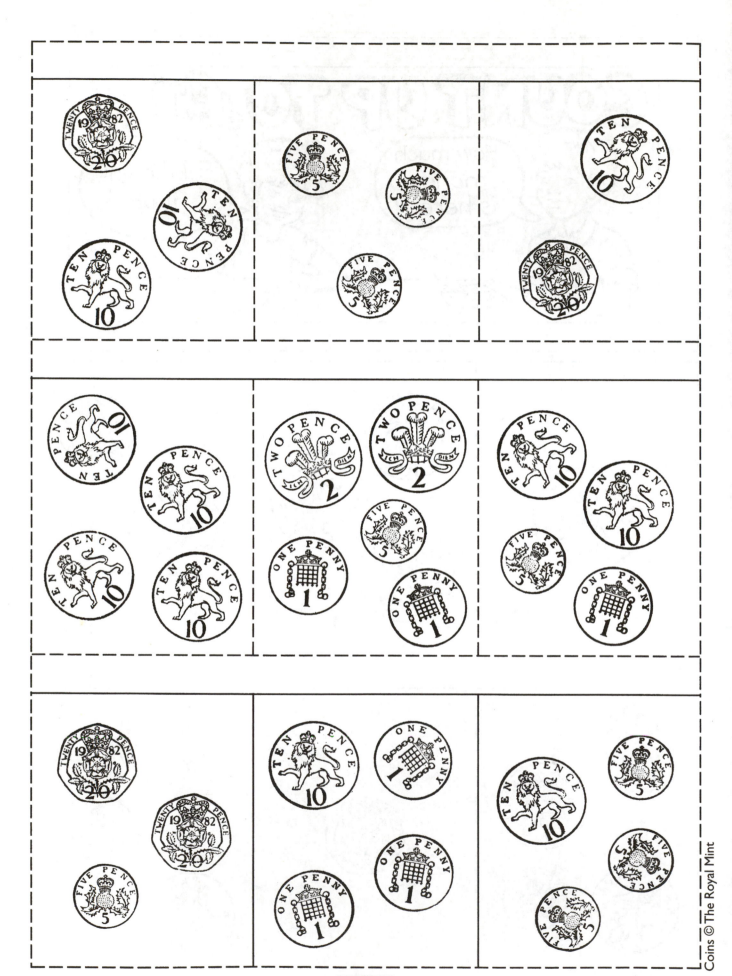

Coins © The Royal Mint

SCHOLASTIC
www.scholastic.co.uk

Name _____

Holidays

◆ Ask your friends which one of these places they would like to go to for their holidays.

◆ Use the boxes to show which place they choose.

NO FUSS
PHOTOCOPIABLE

Holiday homes

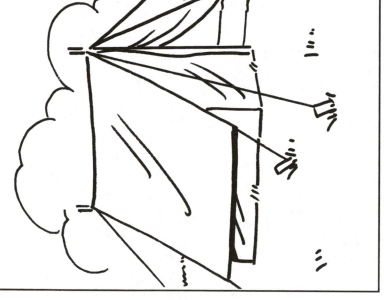

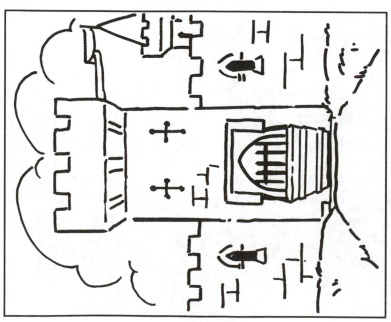

◆ Ask your friends which one of these homes they would like to live in on holiday.

◆ Use the boxes to show which home they choose.

SCHOLASTIC
www.scholastic.co.uk

Choose a badge

◆ Draw 4 badge designs.
◆ Ask your friends which badge they like the most.

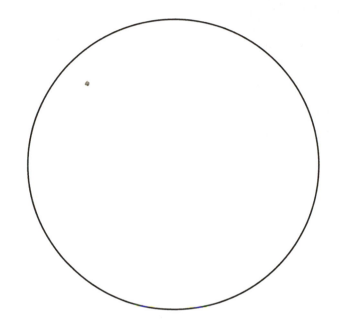
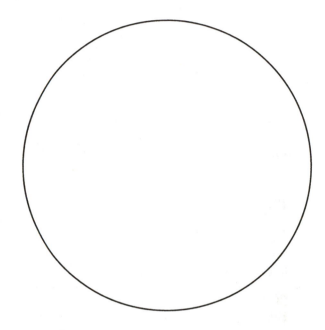
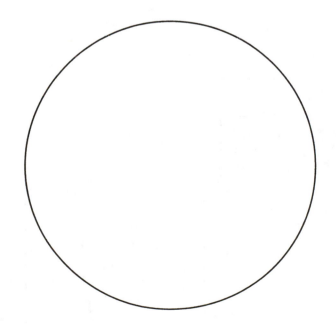
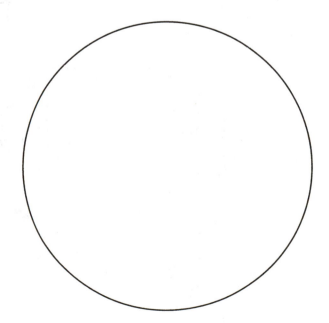

Choose your pets

- ◆ Draw yourself in the circle.
- ◆ Draw an extra animal in the square.
- ◆ Tick the animals you would choose as pets.

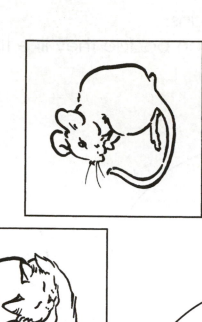

Name _____

Shoes

✤ Look at the shoes worn by the people in your class. Collect information about the different types of shoes you can see. How many people wear each type of shoe?

✤ Make a chart or table to show what you have found out.

number of children
wearing type of shoe
↑

15				
14				
13				
12				
11				
10				
9				
8				
7				
6				
5				
4				
3				
2				
1				

→ types of shoe

www.scholastic.co.uk

Free choice

✿ A class decided to find out what was the favourite 'free choice' activity. They carried out a survey of every child in the class. This is the way they recorded their findings.

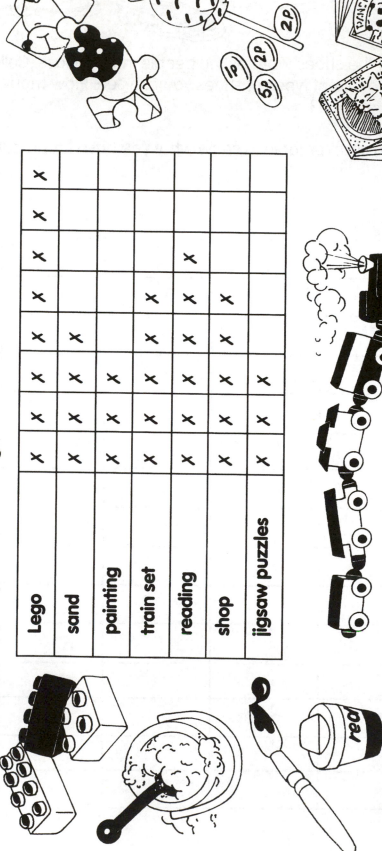

Lego	x	x	x	x	x	x	x	x
sand	x	x	x	x	x			
painting	x	x	x	x				
train set	x	x	x	x	x			
reading	x	x	x	x	x	x	x	
shop	x	x	x	x				
jigsaw puzzles	x	x	x					

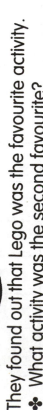

They found out that Lego was the favourite activity.

✿ What activity was the second favourite?

✿ How many children did they ask?

✿ Carry out a survey in your class to find out the most popular free-choice activity.

Name _____

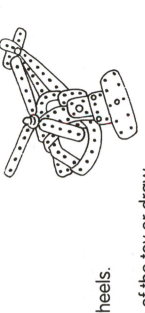

Is and is not

♣ Make a collection of toys for sorting. Include some metal toys that have wheels.

♣♣ Think about the different ways of sorting these toys.

♣ Look at this chart. Which toys would go into each section? Write the name of the toy or draw a picture of it in the correct part of the chart.

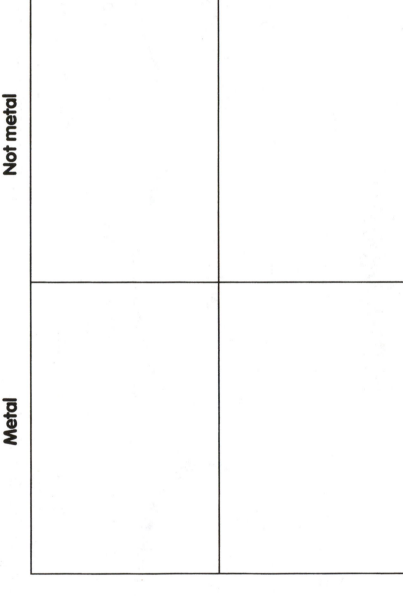

	Metal	Not metal
Wheels		
No wheels		

How likely?

* Cut along the dotted lines.
* Sort the statements into three piles, one pile for each category.

certain

uncertain

impossible

* Make up 2 more statements of your own to go into each category and write them on the blank strips.

Tomorrow the sun will rise.

I will get some new clothes this month.

I will be three years older by tomorrow morning.

Tomorrow I will be younger than I am today.

Tomorrow the sun will shine.

My old clothes will wear out.

NO FUSS PHOTOCOPIABLE

■SCHOLASTIC
www.scholastic.co.uk

Games

I asked 20 children if they knew how to play these games and I kept a tally.
How many children played each game?

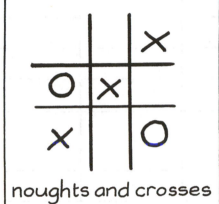

noughts and crosses

dominoes

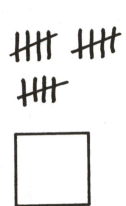

snakes and ladders

snap

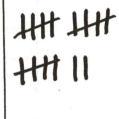

draughts

chess

Name _____

Games graph

Record the information from the games survey on this graph.

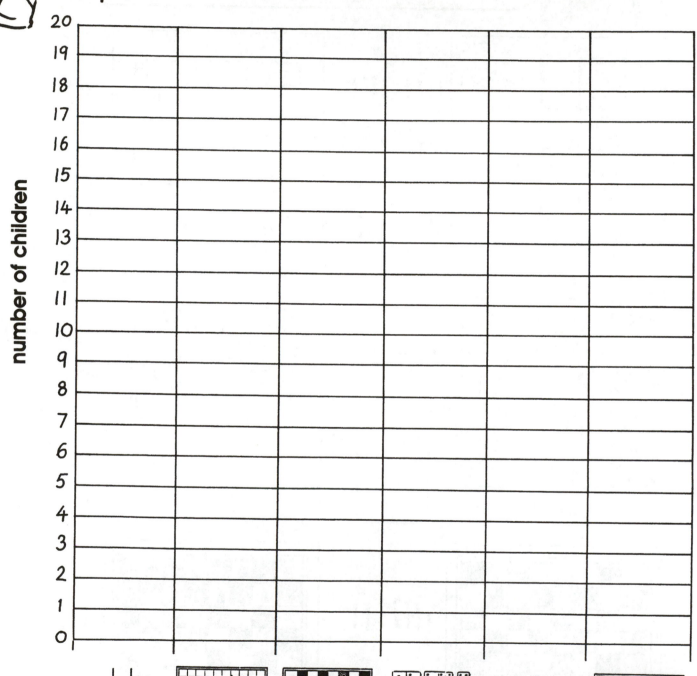

number of children

20
19
18
17
16
15
14
13
12
11
10
9
8
7
6
5
4
3
2
1
0

games

 **SCHOLASTIC**
www.scholastic.co.uk

Name _____

Shape sets

❧ Look at these sets.

❧ For each set, draw a cross (✗) on the shape that does not belong.

❧ Draw another set of shapes here.

❧ Ask a friend to find the shape that does not belong.

Matching

You will need: a pencil, a set of 2-D shapes.

✤ Find a 2-D shape for each picture.

✤ Draw a line from each shape to its label.

rectangle

triangle

square

rectangle

circle

circle

Name _____

Shape jigsaws

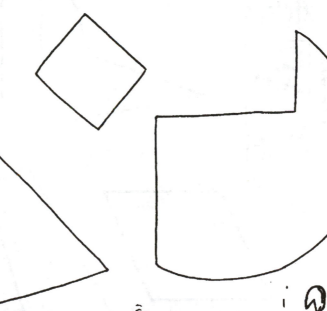

Cut ✂

You will need: scissors, paste, paper.

✤ Cut out the shapes.

✤ Paste them together to make:

- a circle
- a rectangle
- a triangle
- a square

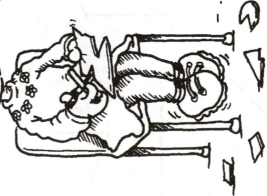

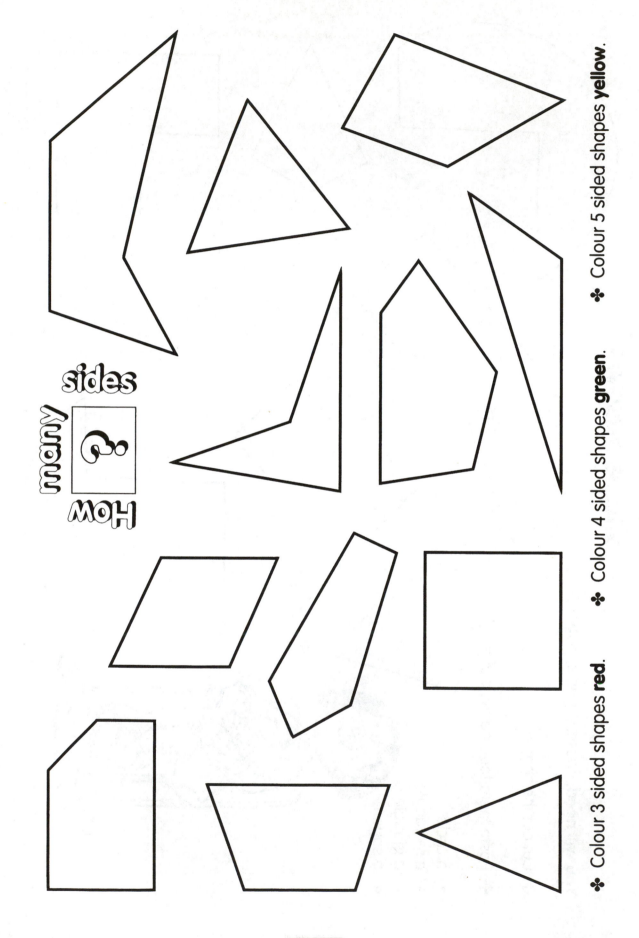

How many sides ?

* Colour 5 sided shapes **yellow**.

* Colour 4 sided shapes **green**.

* Colour 3 sided shapes **red**.

SCHOLASTIC
www.scholastic.co.uk

Shape game – 1

Shape game – 2

Cut along the dotted lines.

Sort the shapes.

Name _____

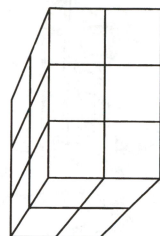

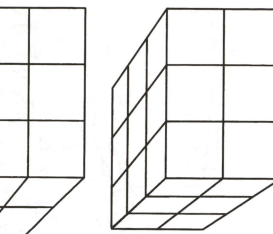

Building with cubes

You will need: a pencil, a set of linking cubes such as Multilink or Unifix.

♣ Make this shape with the cubes.

♣ I have used ☐ cubes.

♣ Can you make any other shapes with the same number of cubes?

♣ Make this shape with the cubes.

♣ I have used ☐ cubes.

♣ Can you make any other shapes with the same number of cubes?

♣ Make this shape with the cubes.

♣ I have used ☐ cubes.

♣ Can you make any other shapes with the same number of cubes?

NO FUSS
PHOTOCOPIABLE

$100 - 50 = 50$
$30 \times 30 = 900$
$20 \times 20 =$

3-D search

❖ Look for cubes, cuboids, cylinders and spheres in your classroom.

❖ Draw or list the objects in the correct boxes.

▱ cube	▱ cuboid	▱ cylinder	○ sphere

Name _____

More matching

♣ Find a 3-D shape for each picture.   ♣ Draw a line from each shape to its label.

You will need: a pencil, a set of 3-D shapes.

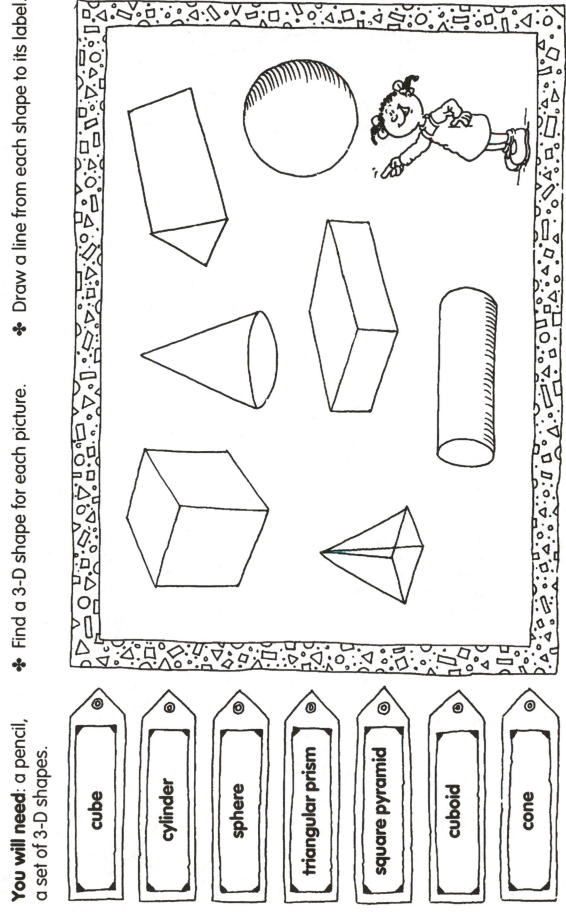

cube

cylinder

sphere

triangular prism

square pyramid

cuboid

cone

Name

Shape sorting

♣ Cut along the dotted lines. Which shapes do you think are the same in some way. Why?
♣ Find at least three different ways to sort the shapes. Record what you have done.
♣ Make some shapes of your own to sort.

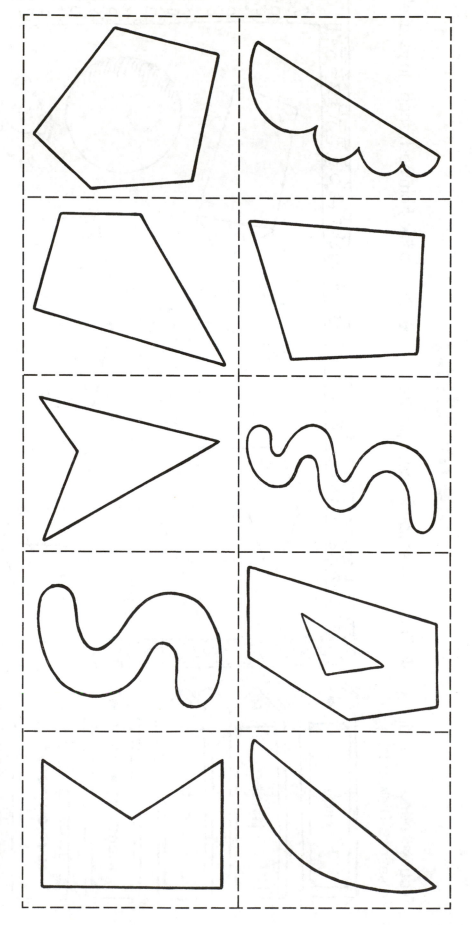

Name _____

Repeating shapes

✤ Continue these patterns:

✤ Make some patterns of your own with shapes like these:

Name _____

Shipshapes

Here are a square and two right-angled triangles.

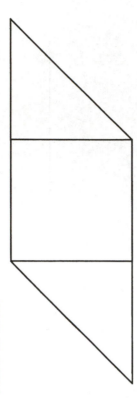

✿ What other shapes can you make?

✿ What shapes can you make when you can only match together edges that are the same length? Here is one:

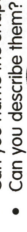

✿ Find some shapes like these, or cut them out of card.

This is one shape picture that you can make with them:

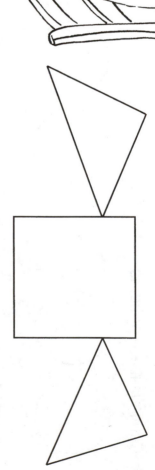

• How many can you make?
• Can you name the shapes you make?
• Can you describe them?

Name _____

Shopping shapes

You will need: some solid shapes and some empty boxes and containers.

Here are some items from a shopping bag.

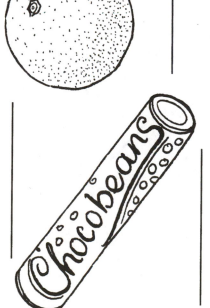

❖ Find a solid shape to match each item.
❖ Write the name of the shape underneath each item.
❖ What other shapes can you find to match things which may be in a shopping bag?
❖ Make a collection of different-shaped packages.

NO FUSS
PHOTOCOPIABLE

3-D structures

❖ Get a set of three-dimensional (3-D) shapes.
❖ Look carefully at the drawings below and find the shapes which match each one.

Draw your structure here.

❖ Use all of these shapes to make a structure. Try and draw what you have made.

Name _____

The maze

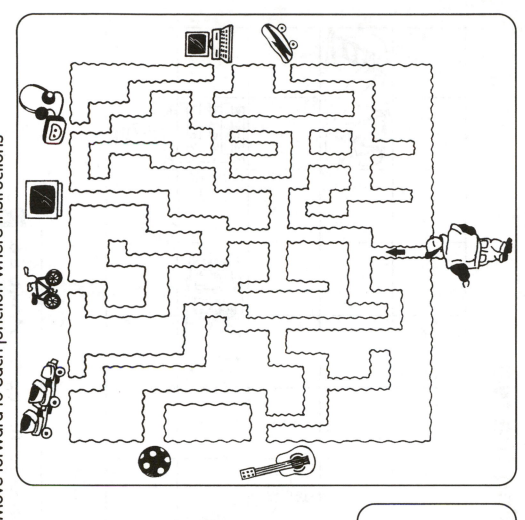

❖ Imagine you are walking through the maze. What do you think you will reach when you get out?

❖ Follow the instructions to get through the maze. Move forward to each junction where instructions are given for your next move.

F means move **forward**
L means turn **left**
R means turn **right**

F. R. F. L. F. R. F. R. F. L. F. L. F. F. R. F. R. L. F.

Remember to stop at each junction before following the next instruction.

❖ Write instructions below to get from the start to a different prize.

Name _____

Finding the way

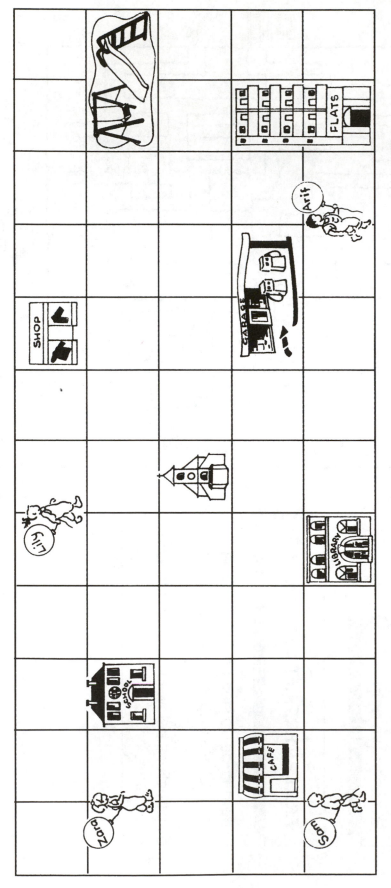

✿ For Sam to get to the adventure playground he has to:

Go forward 4. Turn left at the library. Go forward 3. Turn right. Go forward 6.

✿ Write the route instructions for each child to reach the adventure playground.

✿ Draw two more children onto this street grid and write instructions for them too.

Name _____

Caterpillars

You will need: scissors, paste.

These two caterpillars are the same length.

❖ Cut out the four caterpillars at the bottom of the page.

❖ Paste each one below the caterpillar that is the same length.

Paste

Paste

Paste

Paste

Cut

As long as

You will need: interlocking cubes such as Unifix or Multilink, Plasticine, a pencil.

✤ Join cubes to make a snake as long as each of these:

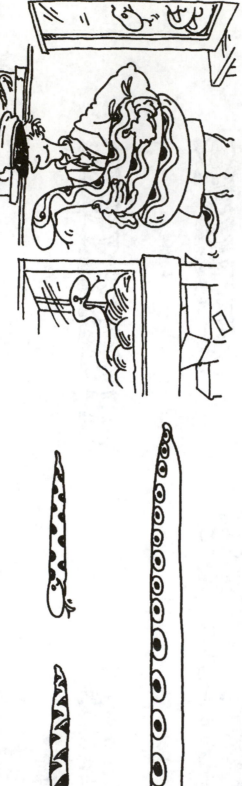

✤ Use Plasticine to make a snake as long as your thumb.

✤ Use Plasticine to make the longest snake you can.

✤ Compare it with some of your friends' snakes.
Who made the longest snake? _____

Aliens

Draw another alien here.

You will need: coloured pencils, scissors, paste, paper.

❖ Look carefully at these aliens.
♣ Colour the shortest alien blue.
Colour the tallest alien red.

Cut ✂

❖ Cut out all the aliens.

❖ Put them in order of height, from shortest to tallest.
♣ Paste them on to a sheet of paper in this order.

Smaller than your hand

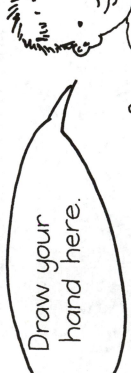

Now draw 4 things that are smaller than your hand.

Draw your hand here.

What shall I use?

You will need: building blocks, straws, a piece of string, a pencil.

These things can all be used for measuring length:

blocks

straws

string

strides

❊ Measure the items listed in the table.
Choose the most appropriate measuring device from those shown above.

❊ Write your answers in the table.

Item to be measured	Measuring device used	Answer	Did you choose the most appropriate measuring device? Explain.
length of a desk/table			
width of a book			
my wrist			
distance to lunch room			
length of a pencil			
height of a chair			

Measuring with hands and feet

These pictures show some of the different ways in which we can use parts of our bodies for measuring.

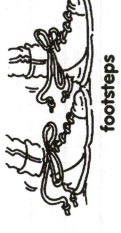

handspans

strides

footsteps

fingerspaces

✿ Measure the items listed in the table, using the most appropriate body part.

✿ Write your answers in the table.

✿ Choose five other items to measure.

✿ Write your answers in the table.

✿ Compare your answers with those of your friends.

Were your answers the same? _____
Why?/Why not?

_____
_____
_____

Item to be measured	Body part used	Answer
length of a pencil		
height of a desk/table		
distance from my desk/table to the teacher's desk		
width of a door		
distance from classroom to school office		

Name _____

Weigh the apple

Put an apple in one bucket. Find things which balance with the apple and draw them.

NO FUSS
PHOTOCOPIABLE

Name _____

Using a balance

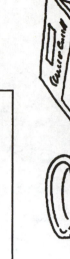
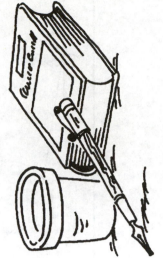

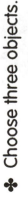

You will need: a collection of small objects, a balance, a pencil.

✤ Choose three objects.

✤ Draw them in the boxes.

✤ Pick up each object in turn and then answer these questions:

   ● Which do you think is the heaviest? _____

   ● Which do you think is the lightest? _____

✤ Use a balance to weigh each object in turn.

✤ Draw them again, putting them in order from lightest to heaviest.

lightest

heaviest

✤ Were your guesses correct? _____

■■SCHOLASTIC
www.scholastic.co.uk

Name _____

Blocks

You will need: a balance, some blocks, a collection of small objects, a pencil.

❖ Put each object in turn on one end of the balance.

❖ Estimate how many blocks it will take to balance the object.

❖ Use blocks to check your estimate.

❖ Record your work on the scales below.

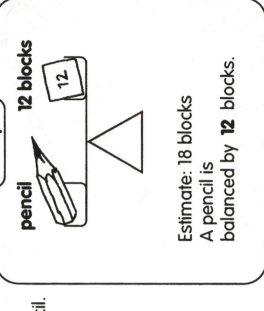

Example:

pencil · 12 blocks

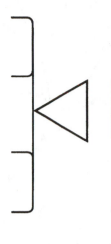

Estimate: 18 blocks
A pencil is
balanced by **12** blocks.

Estimate: ☐ blocks

A _____ is
balanced by ☐ blocks.

Estimate: ☐ blocks

A _____ is
balanced by ☐ blocks.

Estimate: ☐ blocks

A _____ is
balanced by ☐ blocks.

❖ Which object was the heaviest? _____

Which object was the lightest? _____

My shoe

You will need: a balance, a collection of small objects, a pencil.

✤ Put your shoe on one end of the balance.

✤ Try balancing your shoe with different objects in turn.

✤ Write or draw the objects which balance your shoe in the circles below.

My shoe is balanced by...

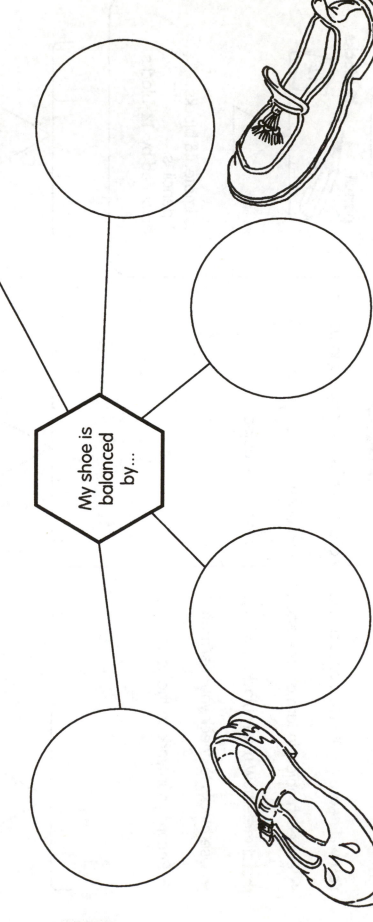

SCHOLASTIC
www.scholastic.co.uk

Bottles

Count how many yoghurt pots of water it takes to fill each bottle.

Find 3 bottles and draw them here.

————— yoghurt pots

————— yoghurt pots

————— yoghurt pots

NO FUSS
PHOTOCOPIABLE

Sand

Find a bottle to fill with sand.

Record how many spoonfuls of sand it took to fill your bottle.	
Record how many cupfuls of sand it took to fill your bottle.	
Record how many yoghurt pots full of sand it took to fill your bottle.	

Name _____

Night and day

You will need: scissors.

✤ Look at these pictures.
Do they show night or day?

✤ Cut out the pictures.

✤ Sort them into two sets: 'Night' and 'Day'.

Cut ✂

Name _____

O'clock

A game for two or more players

You will need: scissors.

- Cut out the cards.
- Place the cards face down.
- Each player in turn turns up two cards.
- If they match, the player keeps them and has another turn.
- If not, turn them back face down and it is the next player's turn.
- The winner is the player with the most pairs when all the cards have been used up.

Cut ✂

| 6 o'clock | 5 o'clock | 4 o'clock | 3 o'clock | 2 o'clock | 1 o'clock |
| 12 o'clock | 11 o'clock | 10 o'clock | 9 o'clock | 8 o'clock | 7 o'clock |

SCHOLASTIC
www.scholastic.co.uk

Name _____

The seasons

You will need: paper, a ruler, a pencil, scissors, paste.

✦ On a large sheet of paper, draw four columns and label them like this:

Summer	Autumn	Winter	Spring

✦ Cut out the pictures below and paste each one in the correct column.

✦ Draw another picture in each column.

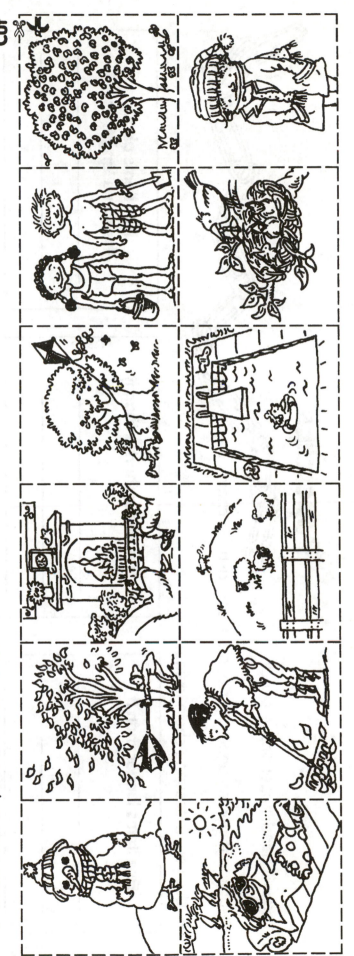

Cut

Name _____

Paperclips

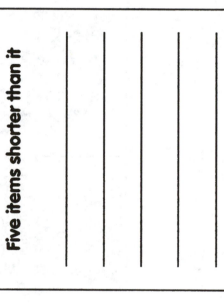

You will need: paperclips, a pencil.

✣ Link together ten paperclips to make a measuring chain.

✣ Use your measuring chain to find:

Five items longer than it	Five items shorter than it	Five items about the same length as it

✣ List the items in the boxes.

✣ Join your measuring chain to that of a friend.

✣ Use your new long measuring chain to find three items longer than it, three items shorter than it and three items about the same length as it.

✣ Record your work on the back of this sheet.

Name _____

A metre

You will need: a 1m string, a ½m string, a pencil.

✤ Use a 1m string to measure the items listed in the table.

✤ Complete the table by placing a tick (✓) in the most appropriate column.

Item to be measured	More than 1m	Less than 1m	About 1m
my height			
around a PE hoop			
length of a chalkboard			
width of a window			
height of a doorway			
width of a door			
height of school fence			

✤ Make another list of items to be measured on the back of this sheet.

✤ Use a ½m string to measure them.

✤ State whether each item measures more than ½m, less than ½m or about ½m.

Snails

You will need: a centimetre ruler, a pencil.

In this snail race, the snail that covered the greatest distance was the winner.

✤ Use a ruler to measure the distance covered by each snail.

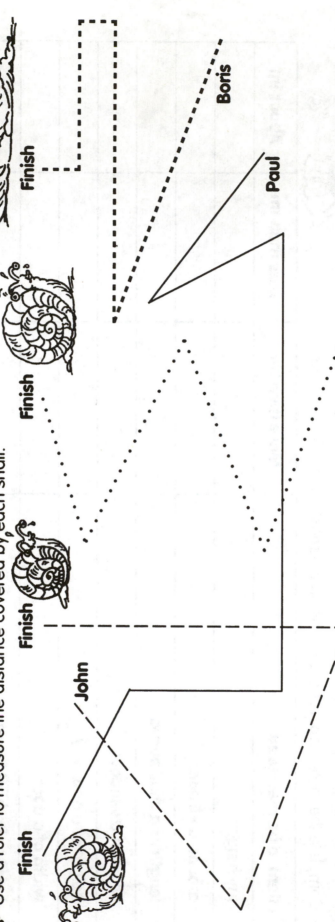

Finish

Finish

Finish

Finish

John

Boris

Paul

Bill

✤ Which snail won the race? _____

✤ Put the snails in order from first to fourth.

1st _____ 2nd _____ 3rd _____ 4th _____

Kilograms

! Take care with plastic bags.

You will need: a 1kg weight, a balance, two plastic bags, a large spoon, some sand.

✤ Use the 1kg weight and the balance to measure out 1kg of sand.

✤ Put the sand in a plastic bag.

✤ Use the 1kg of sand and the balance to find:

Three objects that weigh about 1kg

1 _____
2 _____
3 _____

Three objects that weigh less than 1kg

1 _____
2 _____
3 _____

Three objects that weigh more than 1kg

1 _____
2 _____
3 _____

✤ Use your 1kg bag of sand and the balance to make a ½kg bag of sand.

✤ Explain what you did. _____

✤ Use your ½kg bag of sand and the balance to find:

Three objects that weigh about ½kg

1 _____
2 _____
3 _____

Three objects that weigh less than ½kg

1 _____
2 _____
3 _____

Three objects that weigh more than ½kg

1 _____
2 _____
3 _____

NO FUSS PHOTOCOPIABLE

Make a metre

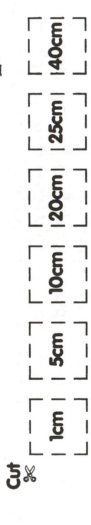

A game for two players

You will need: a metre ruler, a centimetre ruler, scissors, card, coloured pencils, a Multilink or Unifix cube, sticky tape.

• Work with a partner.

• Use the metre ruler to make a 1m strip from card.

• Use these labels and some sticky tape to turn your cube into a dice.

Cut ✂

| 1cm | 5cm | 10cm | 20cm | 25cm | 40cm |

• Player 1 throws the dice and marks the distance shown (using a centimetre ruler) on the metre strip.

• Player 2 then has a turn, marking the distance in a different colour, and so on.

• The winner is the first person to 'make a metre'.

SCHOLASTIC
www.scholastic.co.uk

The estimating game

A game for two or more players

You will need: paper, pencils, a range of measuring devices, scissors.

- Cut out the cards.
- Place the cards face down on the table.
- A card is chosen and each player records his or her estimate of the answer.
- The object is then measured and a point is awarded to the player with the closest estimate.
- The winner is the player with the most points when all the cards have been used.

✂ Cut

How long is the chalkboard?	**Draw a line 8cm long without using a ruler.**	**Who is the tallest person in your class?**	**How high is a desk?**
What is the length of a pencil?	**Cut a piece of string 1¼m long.**	**How wide is the doorway?**	**What is the perimeter of the playing field?**
Cut a piece of paper into a rectangular shape 18 cm × 6cm.	**How far can one of you jump?**	**What is the height of your teacher's desk?**	**How long is a shoelace?**
How long is your teacher's signature?	**How high is the ceiling?**	**How long is a tie?**	**How many metres is it to the school office?**

Changing shape

You will need: a balance, Plasticine, some blocks, a pencil.

✤ Take a lump of Plasticine and make it into a ball shape.

✤ Weigh the Plasticine using some blocks.

✤ Record how many blocks it takes to balance the Plasticine in the first box.

✤ Now make the same lump of Plasticine into five different shapes in turn.

✤ Use blocks to weigh each shape.

✤ Record your work in the other boxes.

[ ] blocks balance the Plasticine.

[ ] blocks balance the Plasticine.

[ ] blocks balance the Plasticine.

[ ] blocks balance the Plasticine.

[ ] blocks balance the Plasticine.

[ ] blocks balance the Plasticine.

✤ Discuss your answers with a friend and write down what you have discovered.

Predicting

a level cup

You will need: a cup, a balance, weights, some water, some sand, some rice, some pasta, some rice crispies.

✤ Think about how much a level cup of each of the above substances will weigh.

✤ List them in order from lightest to heaviest.

My predictions		After weighing
lightest	1 _____	1 _____
	2 _____	2 _____
	3 _____	3 _____
	4 _____	4 _____
heaviest	5 _____	5 _____

Substance	Weight
a cup of water	
a cup of sand	
a cup of rice	
a cup of pasta	
a cup of rice crispies	

✤ Now weigh a level cup of each substance to check your predictions.

✤ List them in order from lightest to heaviest.

✤ Were your predictions correct? _____

Explain. _____

✤ Which substance was the heaviest? _____

✤ Which substance was the lightest? _____

Grams

1kg = 1000g

You will need: a balance, a collection of small objects, a pencil.

✤ Make a list of ten small objects in the table.

✤ Estimate the weight, in grams, of each object.

✤ Weigh each object in grams.

✤ Convert your answers to kilograms (and grams).

✤ List the objects in order from lightest to heaviest.

Object	Estimated weight (g)	Actual weight (g)	Actual weight (kg)

lightest →→→ heaviest

Name _____

Full or empty?

You will need: some old magazines, a pencil.

✤ Look at this picture.

✤ Draw a cross (**X**) on each container that is empty.

✤ Draw a circle (**O**) round each container that is full.

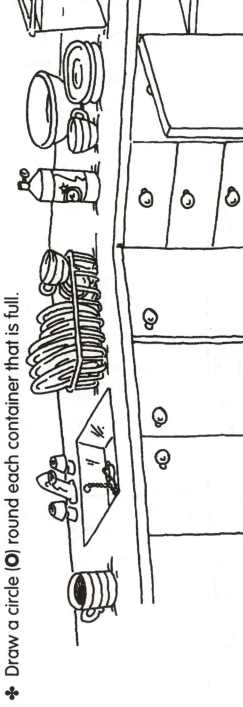

✤ Look through a magazine to find some 'full'/'empty' pictures.

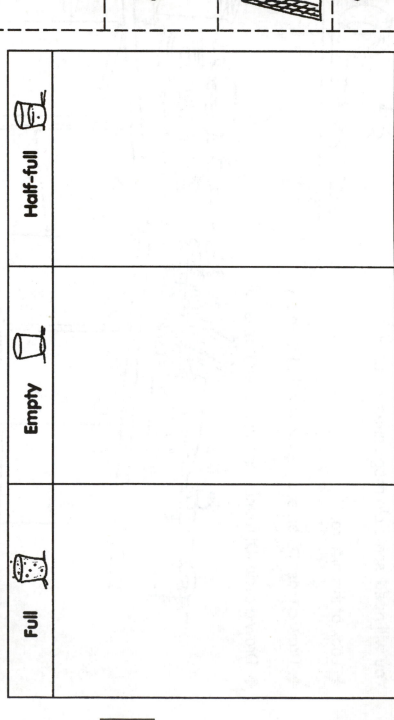

Half-full

You will need: scissors, paste, a pencil.

✿ Look at each of the pictures on the right and decide whether the container shown is full, half-full or empty.

✿ Cut out each picture and paste it in the correct box.

Full	Empty	Half-full

✿ Draw another picture to go in each box.

Name _____

Which holds most?

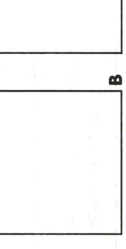
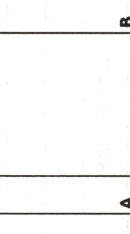

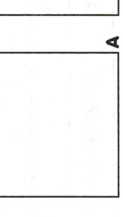

You will need: three different empty containers, some sand, a pencil, scissors, paper, sticky tape.

♣ Label the containers **A**, **B** and **C**.

♣ Draw them in these boxes.

♣ Which container do you think will hold the most?

♣ Which container do you think will hold the least?

♣ Do you think any of them will hold the same amount?

_____

♣ Check your predictions by pouring.

♣ Draw the containers again, this time in order, starting with the container which holds the least.

C   **B**   **A**

most   least

Name _____

Litres

You will need: a large empty bottle, some other empty containers, a 1l jug, paper, sticky tape, scissors, a pencil.

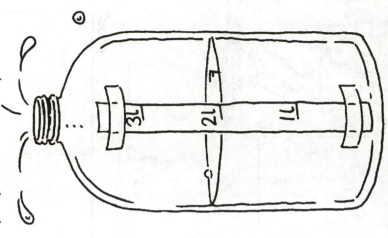

❖ Cut out a strip of paper and tape it to the large bottle.

❖ Using the 1l jug, pour 1l of water into the bottle.

❖ Mark the level on the paper strip.

❖ Repeat this procedure until the bottle is full.

❖ Use your litre measure to find the capacity of several other containers.

❖ Record your estimate of the capacity of each one first.

These words will help you:
a bit more than
a bit less than
about halfway between
about equal to

Container	Estimated capacity (l)	Actual capacity (l)

SCHOLASTIC
www.scholastic.co.uk

Name _____

Make a litre

You will need: a pencil, a 1l container, five smaller containers (for example, an eggcup, a plastic cup, a pill bottle, a yoghurt pot).

✤ In turn, use each small container to fill the 1l container.

✤ Draw how many times you had to fill the small container.

✤ Which of the small containers was the easiest to use? _____ Why? _____

✤ If you had to fill a 5l container, which of the small containers would you use? _____ Why? _____

In a minute

You will need: coloured pencils, a 1-minute timer, a ball.

♣ Work with a partner.

♣ Try each of these activities for 1 minute.

♣ Your partner will time you.

♣ Before you start, write your predictions in red pencil.

♣ Record your actual results in blue pencil.

♣ Make up another activity to complete in 1 minute.

♣ Record your results in the empty box.

I can count to _____ in 1 minute.

I can say the alphabet _____ times in 1 minute.

I can bounce a ball _____ times in 1 minute.

I can write my name _____ times in 1 minute.

I can run _____ times round the field in 1 minute.

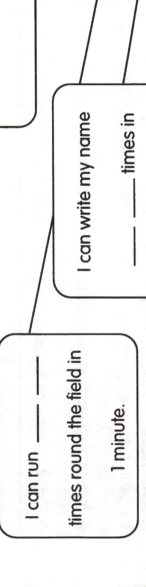

1 minute

SCHOLASTIC
www.scholastic.co.uk

Name _____

Seconds

You will need: a stopwatch, a pencil.

✤ Work with a partner.

✤ Use the stopwatch to time each activity.

✤ Before you start, write down your predictions.

✤ Then record your actual results.

Name of activity	Prediction (seconds)	Time taken (seconds)
write my name five times		
tie my shoelace		
put on my jacket		
take off my shoes and socks		
say the alphabet		

✤ Think of some more activities to complete the table.

SCHOLASTIC

In this series:

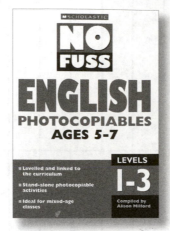

ISBN 0-439-96548-9
ISBN 978-0439-96548-4

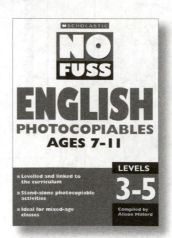

ISBN 0-439-96549-7
ISBN 978-0439-96549-1

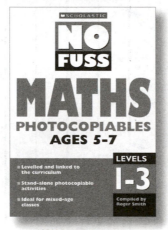

ISBN 0-439-96550-0
ISBN 978-0439-96550-7

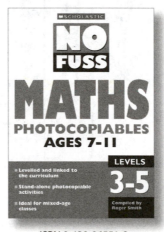

ISBN 0-439-96551-9
ISBN 978-0439-96551-4

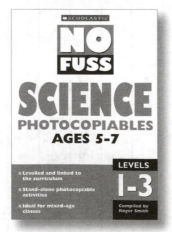

ISBN 0-439-96552-7
ISBN 978-0439-96552-1

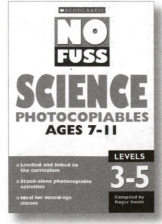

ISBN 0-439-96553-5
ISBN 978-0439-96553-8

To find out more, call: 0845 603 9091
or visit our website www.scholastic.co.uk